To all members of the <u>Chicago</u> Federation <u>of</u>
Musicians:

This book <u>THE MUSICIANS</u> and <u>PETRILLO</u> is sent to
you with the compliments of the Chicago Federation
of Musicians by order of the Board of Directors
of Local No. 10.

                    Fraternally yours,

                    Edward A Benkert

                    Recording Secretary

JAMES CAESAR PETRILLO

The Musicians and Petrillo

By
ROBERT D. LEITER

BOOKMAN ASSOCIATES, INC.
NEW YORK

145

To the memories of

my mother, GUSSIE

and

my father, J. HESCHEL

CONTENTS

CONTENTS

PREFACE

The story of the musicians union is a study in personalities, power, and technological change. For more than half a century the union of musicians—the American Federation of Musicians— has been dominated by forceful leaders who, when they desired, have imposed their wishes upon the organization. These men generally have adhered scrupulously to the laws and rules of the union; but at the same time the laws have been so formulated that the international president has been able, if he deemed it necessary, to balk the desires of the majority of the members.

The power of the union is evident not only in the internal affairs of the organization, but in the union's relations with employers. The American Federation of Musicians exercises complete control over professional musicians in the United States. A musician who is not in the union normally cannot earn a livelihood by playing an instrument. The union frequently has been able to impose the terms of employment upon employers without negotiation. Some employers and some agents have been required to secure licenses from the union before being able to hire or deal with musicians.

The judicial functions performed by the AFM have made it unnecessary and unusual for members or employers to appeal to the courts. Claims are collected for members or employers, fines are imposed, and regulations are enforced. The ability of the union to expel a member or to put an employer on the unfair list and thereby make it impossible for him to obtain the services of musicians has proved sufficiently effective in enforcing its decisions.

Inventions have changed the forms and types of music which the public hears. These technological advances have impinged on the employment opportunities of musicians and have raised problems and issues which have been the concern of the public for many years. The activities of musicians are closely connected with the entertainment industry and have therefore aroused more popular interest than the work of most other laborers. Only

8

during the last few years, however, has some progress been made in solving a few of these problems.

This book traces the development and growth of the union as an economic force. It begins with the earliest attempts to unionize musicians in the United States and carries the narrative to the present time. It considers the various problems which arose, the impact of the actions of musicians on other sectors of the economy, and the personalities of the men who shaped the destiny of the union. Throughout its existence, the American Federation of Musicians has been involved in a competitive struggle. At first organized musicians were faced with the competition of the nonunionized instrumentalists. When this problem was essentially solved, it was replaced by the more serious and complicated one involving the competitive force of technology.

This study was made over a period of several years. It involved a careful examination of every issue of the monthly newspapers of the international union and of the New York local, of the periodicals of several other locals, and of official documents released by the union. Clipping files and newspaper indexes were consulted. Numerous magazine articles dealing with the musicians and with James Caesar Petrillo were studied. All the Congressional hearings and reports connected with this union were analyzed. Relevant publications issued by trade associations and by interested employers were read. Many books were checked for pertinent information.

Scores of conferences and interviews were held with representatives of management, with elected and appointed officials of the international union and of several locals, and with persons interested in music. Many working musicians, some of whom were my students at the time of the discussions, supplied various types of information. To all of these persons, a great number of whom have asked to remain anonymous, I express my gratitude.

R.D.L.

City College of New York
June 1, 1953

THE MUSICIANS FORM A UNION • 1

"... by far the most marked progress our organization
has made was made by reason of its readiness to confer
with the employer and settle controversies over the conference table."

JOSEPH NICHOLAS WEBER

• The Place of the Musician in the Nineteenth Century

Musicians represent a respected group in the labor force today,
but they did not always enjoy such status. For centuries musicians, along with actors, magicians, acrobats, hypnotists, and
other performers, in general, were regarded as peculiar persons.
The ability to play an instrument was considered by many people
to be strange. The public was especially suspicious of those men
who supplemented their musical performance with other feats
in order to earn a livelihood. Such cases were not unusual. An
application letter from a musician written during the Middle
Ages and preserved at Oxford University says: "I can play the
lute and the pipe, the harp, the organistrum, the bagpipe and
the tabor. I can throw knives and catch them without cutting
myself. I can tell a tale against any man and make love verses for
the ladies. I can move tables and juggle the chairs. I can turn
somersaults and stand on my head."[1]
Musicians were looked upon askance in the United States
throughout the nineteenth century. Since then, however, their
prestige has risen. A number of factors have been responsible for
the change.
A competent musician had to have both talent and skill. Yet
before the twentieth century, only in rare cases was he able to
make a living by working solely as a musician. Employment opportunities were not good. Permanent symphony orchestras
were found only in a few of the largest cities. There were not
many big bands, and several of those in existence were found in
state penitentiaries. Musicians were limited essentially to playing
at dances, picnics, serenades, and funerals.

The struggle by musicians to improve their economic status was similar in many ways to those engaged in by other workers; but in various respects it had its own characteristics. Music at first was not classified either as a trade or as a profession. But musicians formed labor associations by the second half of the nineteenth century and in this regard they acted like other skilled workers.

Unskilled workers usually lacked the education, intelligence, experience, and energy, to set up permanent organizations for their own advantage. Workers with skills had higher standards of living and more opportunity to examine their status and plan for the advancement of their interests. The craftsmen in the larger cities were the first to form labor unions.

These unions, however, did not have the same purposes as those in existence today. Twentieth-century trade unions are concerned mainly with the improvement of wages, hours, and conditions of work. During the first part of the nineteenth century the right of workers to engage in such activities was not established legally. Concerted demands upon employers often were considered conspiracies in restraint of trade. The first labor unions therefore were social organizations. Frequently, they functioned as mutual insurance organizations and members would be entitled to sick benefits, death benefits, and unemployment benefits. By the middle of the century rulings of the judiciary established the right of workers to organize and exert economic strength in order to improve their economic position.

Shoemakers, carpenters, printers, and tailors established labor organizations. Professional groups like teachers, lawyers, and doctors, even when employed by others, were not affected by unionization. Feelings of independence and of being able to advance through the exercise of initiative always have dominated the thinking of professional employees. During the nineteenth century musicians stood midway between these groups.

The long period of training and experience necessary to perform satisfactorily on an instrument provided an aspect of professionalism to the work of musicians. Manual skills and dexterity had to be present but they were subordinate to musical instinct and intuition. Yet as in the case of other skilled workers, the greatest efficiency of the musician, especially on wind instruments, usually is achieved at a comparatively early age. The con-

ditions surrounding the economic life of the musician were unfavorable and the opportunities for improving his status were
limited. The standards and codes of the nineteenth century
frowned upon the work of the musician. Entertainers were sup-
posed to represent an inferior social class and they were shunned
in the social intercourse of the community.

Though rapid movement from one social class to another was
still possible, the establishment of trade unions was one of the
first signs of more rigid stratification of classes; it marked the
acceptance of this condition by the wage earners. Many musicians
liked to think that they were part of a professional class but they
were not completely correct because the public was not impressed
with their qualifications. The audience usually expected the
musician to perform a vaudeville act as well as to play an instrument.

Orchestras were expected to take part in minstrel shows. Musicians blackened their faces and became end men and jesters.
Music was a public attraction in many parts of the United States
only if it was supplemented by some unusual demonstration. A
pianist would fasten sleigh bells to his legs, bands would rein-
force sound effects with cannon shots, musicians would execute
400 notes in one measure, or singers would sing 600 words and
300 bars of music in four minutes. Freak stunts were part of the
usual routine by which musicians earned a living. During the
nineteenth century, most of the musicians who stuck to music
only, were barely able to eke out an existence. They played at
picnics, in theater pits, in churches, at grange halls, in dance
halls, and at parades. Employment was unsteady and conditions
of work were poor.

Generally, musicians have no permanent employer but constantly are seeking new jobs. In this respect the work of musicians
is different from that of employees in other fields where the employer hires workers for relatively long periods of time and where
the hours and conditions of work are more regular. Within a short
span of time, a musician may be employed by many men, each
of whom operates a different type of establishment—for example,
theater, night club, restaurant, catering hall, symphony, or fraternal organization. Musicians have to move from one place of
work to another. Usually such travel occurs only within one town
or city but many performers lead an itinerant existence. They

search for employment opportunities throughout the country and thereby create problems for musicians who stay in one locality.

Music differs also from most other occupations in that a large number of musicians are not working as instrumentalists all the time. These men have a regular trade or occupation but play an instrument to add to their incomes. They are known as the semi-professional musicians and are distinguished from the group of professional musicians whose full time normally is devoted to the rendition of music. (Nonprofessional musicians receive no income for their performance.)

These peculiarities of the musical field have led to an unusual method of employing personnel. The hiring system depends upon a contractor. When a band or orchestra is needed for any function or engagement, the employer hires a contractor, who is more familiar with the talent available, to secure the necessary personnel. The musicians are supervised by the contractor and the employer. Formerly, the generally weak economic position of the musician was a severe handicap to him. Since employment was not steady, he was competing constantly with his fellows for the available positions. Straitened circumstances made him willing to accept a lower price and thereby tended to force his wages down. In addition, competition between contractors to secure the engagement from the employer tended to reduce the remuneration of the musician still further because the contractor had less money to distribute among the men. By quoting a lower price to the purchaser of music, the contractor was forced to lower the wage scale of the instrumentalist.

The first musicians unions were not organized to alleviate adverse economic conditions among the membership. These unions comprised the elite among instrumental performers. They maintained an element of exclusiveness by setting rigorous entrance requirements; and inferior performers at first were not admitted to these organizations. An air of fraternalism prevailed in them. Basically they were social clubs where members could get together for discussions and entertainment.

In most of these early unions the German element predominated. Such, for example, was the typical case of the St. Louis local of musicians where an analysis of the national origin of

the 191 members disclosed that in 1888, 78 came from Germany and only 65 were born in the United States. By 1910, however, when the local had 835 members, it was found that 660 of them were born in the United States. Germany fell to the second rank, contributing only 77 members.[2]

A large number of the band and orchestra leaders of that time were saloon keepers.[3] Many members of the bands were recruited from among the beer drinkers in these saloons. In Cincinnati, the local union of musicians was organized as a result of the actions of some of the younger instrumentalists who wished to rid themselves of the arbitrary control exercised by the leaders. These younger men organized a union in order to force the bandmaster to come to them when he needed musicians. In order to further strengthen their position, they also organized a cooperative saloon so that musicians would stay out of the rival establishments (where hiring took place); but this venture was short-lived.

It is true that these unions were interested in the welfare of musicians and would take steps to protect their members if the occasion made such action urgent, but for many years they were concerned mainly with enforcing certain rules applying to benevolent programs which they had set up; a program of death benefits was most typical. The musicians' organizations were interested in presenting programs for the entertainment of the public, planning affairs for their own enjoyment, and engaging in "social hilarity." Only late in the century were attempts made to enforce performance price lists.

Though Baltimore and Chicago had musicians unions as early as 1857, the first organization of a group of musicians whose purposes and objectives were clearly those of a trade union usually is considered to have taken place in New York City. In 1863, under the leadership of Henry D. Beissenherz, a union was formed. The following year, the organization was chartered under the laws of New York State. (It was customary for labor unions to incorporate during that era.) In the succeeding decade, organization was very rapid and many cities in the East and Midwest formed musical unions.

• *National Organizations of Musicians*

The local in Philadelphia took the initiative in 1871 and

called a meeting of the various independent musical unions in the country. It was decided to establish a national organization in order to deal with matters of common interest to musicians and to tackle the problems caused by the competition faced by members of each local from traveling musicians and road shows. The organization, which was known as the National Musical Association, held several conventions, but it endured less than ten years. It never comprised more than 17 locals and its activities were rather limited. It could accomplish nothing because the constituent locals themselves were lacking in authority and power.

By 1885 many unions of musicians had secured a firmer foothold in their jurisdictions and under the leadership of the Cincinnati local a meeting was called for 1886 in New York City. Seven unions were represented—Cincinnati, New York, Philadelphia, Boston, Chicago, Milwaukee, and Detroit—and they agreed to form the National League of Musicians of the United States. The members of the League remained essentially independent locals and retained final authority over all matters in which they were concerned.

The growth of the NLM was rapid. It had 15 locals in 1887, and by 1896, it had 9,000 members in 79 locals. These units were scattered all over the United States. The debates in the conventions held by the League engendered much factional strife and bitterness over the question of whether musicians were artists and professionals or whether they were laborers. Those musicians who claimed they had little in common with workers in manufacturing and construction activity derisively called the other faction "stove polishers," "stove molders," and "shoe makers." The element which considered itself to be laborers called its opponents "silk hats," "toppers," and "Prince Alberts." It was not uncommon for delegates at the annual conventions of the NLM to wear Prince Albert coats, silk hats, and patent leather shoes. In 1887 the NLM voted down a resolution recommended by its president which declared that musicians were "laborers in the field of music."[4]

Affiliation with the American Federation of Labor hinged on this issue. The AFL which had its inception in 1881, was expanding its membership and desired to include all the organized musicians. The Knights of Labor, a rival national organization of workers, which attained its peak membership in the middle of the 1880's, also wanted to enroll the musicians. Individual locals had the choice of joining either the AFL or the Knights, or of remaining independent; and all three alternatives had its adherents. The Knights of Labor, however, soon weakened and became of negligible importance in the labor movement, so that the issue which crystallized for each of the locals was whether or not to join the AFL. Beginning with the second NLM convention, in 1887, the AFL regularly invited the NLM to affiliate with it, but was regularly turned down. The faction opposing affiliation maintained that musicians had little in common with other workers or their unions, and that the musicians union would suffer a loss in dignity and prestige by affiliation. Those men who desired to join the AFL countered with the argument that musicians, like other laborers, were wage earners and that their conditions could be improved more effectively if they combined with the general labor movement. The president of the NLM reported to the 1891 convention: "Concerning the affiliation of the League with the American Federation of Labor, which has been urged repeatedly, thus far without success, those for and against appear to be about evenly divided, with the probability that a majority would favor affiliation, provided it did not involve a surrender of the League's independence. It is a serious question, and the advisability of refraining from committing the League to either side of the questions at issue between Capital and Labor should receive your most earnest consideration."[5]

Although a majority of the locals desired to affiliate, the voting procedure made such a step difficult. The element which opposed affiliation (that is, the group which considered itself professional) was centralized in New York and the other metropolitan areas in the East. It had a much greater membership than the other faction and therefore heavier voting strength in the conventions. Furthermore, the newer Western locals, which were more inclined to affiliate, were generally unable to afford the expenses of delegates and did not send any. The New York local, which opposed affiliation, had from 26 to 30 votes in a convention that never had more than 125 votes.

The American Federation of Labor, therefore, undertook to charter locals of musicians directly, until there would be enough of them so that it could create a national union within its own ranks. By 1895, a large majority of the locals of the NLM were affiliated with the AFL either directly or indirectly. Some of the locals in the League had been chartered directly by the AFL and other unions of musicians were indirectly connected with the AFL through affiliation with the central labor bodies in their respective cities.

•. The American Federation of Musicians

The convention of the AFL in that year authorized President Samuel Gompers to give the NLM one final opportunity to join the AFL. The understanding was that a new national union would be organized if the offer should be rejected. When the NLM, by a tie vote, decided not to join the AFL, Gompers issued a call for a national convention of musicians unions to meet on October 19, 1896. Twenty-six unions representing 24 localities responded to the convention notice by sending either a delegate or a letter. Of these 26, 17 were in the NLM and nine were independent. The delegates represented 4,000 members, 886 of whom were not members of the League.[6] The convention successfully organized the American Federation of Musicians, and received a national charter on November 6, 1896. Owen Miller was elected the first president of the new union.

The AFM desired to avoid jurisdictional difficulties with the NLM. Some of the unions which were independent of the NLM had accepted members from jurisdictions claimed by League locals. In all cases, locals of the NLM were given preference in joining the AFM over other locals in the same areas. Most of the NLM locals were soon members of both organizations. The leaders of the NLM, however, battled those League locals which had joined the American Federation of Musicians. When the 1897 convention of the NLM was held, an attempt was made to bar the delegates from those locals which were also members of the AFM. But the delegates secured a court injunction which ordered the NLM leaders to admit them to the convention. From that time on, the NLM began to decline, and it subsequently never was able to regain its former prestige.

The somewhat prolonged struggle which ensued between the party in the NLM which opposed affiliation, built around the

Musical Mutual Protective Union of New York, and the American Federation of Musicians finally ended with a complete victory by the AFM over the NLM. The National League of Musicians distributed its funds among its component locals and was dissolved at its convention in 1904. "Grand Old Man" Beissenherz, who had been the temporary chairman of the first AFM convention, presided over the final sessions.

The disintegration of the National League of Musicians was not a serious calamity to the musicians. The NLM had failed to assist the locals in improving wages, hours, and other employment conditions. It never had the opportunity to carry out what should have been its chief purposes and functions because it was mainly a forum. The loose nature of its organization, under which the locals retained most of the authority and discretion, did not give it any cohesiveness. The only uniting element in the League was the national death benefit scheme which it had set up and supervised.

The major problem which had faced the NLM was the jealousy and rivalry among the locals. The weaknesses of the League all stemmed from this condition. The attempt to establish a national death benefit scheme which would operate smoothly was a failure. Complaints were leveled against the assessment plan because some locals were receiving more money in benefits than they were paying in as premiums. Such unequal distribution is to be expected under any insurance plan and attitudes of resentment which emerged were not conducive to the satisfactory operation of the plan.

Each local was distrustful of its neighbors and carefully guarded its own jurisdiction. The League required member musicians to seek employment only in their own locality. This rule was desired by the locals and was aimed at keeping musicians out of the jurisdiction of locals other than the one to which they belonged. Each local believed that by building a wall around itself, it would pre-empt the employment opportunities in its own area. But this did not happen because the rule was unenforceable; and it became a dead letter. It was not possible to keep qualified musicians from taking jobs in areas other than their home base when an employer desired to hire them.

The effectiveness of the League was even further curtailed

because there was no provision for an adequate transfer system. Musicians had no simple or convenient way of changing their local affiliation. This worked undue hardships upon them and weakened the structure and value of the NLM. Musicians who found it necessary to move about freely practiced an outright disregard of the rules.

Each union of musicians believed that the device of restricting the membership of the local would benefit its own members. Behind this policy was the mistaken notion that only union musicians were capable of securing employment. The unions refused to recognize their own limitations and weaknesses during this formative period. Before 1900, they almost never had control of any sizable segment of the employers of musicians in any city. The entrance requirements set by the unions, particularly in the East, were designed to exclude musicians rather than select qualified performers. Examinations for admission were discriminatory, arbitrary, and unduly difficult; and initiation fees were exorbitant. Favoritism towards certain nationalities was practiced. It is no wonder that these practices increased rather than lessened competition among musicians. Not only was the existence of a nonunion group encouraged, but rival unions flourished in many cities.

The voting system of the League was poorly devised. Though apparently democratic in that all matters were decided on the basis of a majority of the full membership, the conditions and circumstances of the organization at that time were not propitious to the utilization of this voting procedure. Since the number of votes of each local in the convention was based upon its membership figures, undue advantage was given to certain locals. The few largest musical unions were able to dominate the convention. New York, in combination with a few other Eastern locals, was able to prevail on most issues. This was especially true because the smaller Western locals whose views were closer to those of the general labor movement rarely sent delegates to the conventions. Instead they handed over their proxy votes to the larger locals, which were well represented already. As a result limited interests were served and national considerations were relegated to a position of secondary importance.

It would be a mistake nevertheless to assume that these conditions brought about the end of the NLM and led to the organization of the American Federation of Musicians. Rather the schism between the two groups was mainly the outcome of a political struggle for control. The AFL desired the affiliation of musicians. Some of the leaders in the NLM agreed that this should be done, but others disagreed. In the events which followed, the faction which desired to join the AFL won. There was a change in leadership of the national organization of musicians and nothing more. The American Federation of Musicians, which originally faced the same problems that weakened the NLM, was able to overcome these difficulties. It then began a remarkable career in which the interests of its members substantially were advanced.

The musicians have been fortunate in their leadership, for able and untiring men have always headed the organization. In more than half a century of existence, the destiny of the AFM has been largely in the hands of three men. But all three have been skilled politicians whose policies and tactics, on many occasions better described as machinations and maneuverings, have enabled them to reach and remain at the top of the national union. The first leader was Owen Miller, a forceful individual, who became president of the union when it was founded. His life is interwoven in the development and early growth of trade unionism among musicians.

At an early age Miller was forced to seek employment because of the impoverished condition of his family. The pressure of financial need made it impossible for him to enjoy an education beyond the public schools. But he was a self-taught man and his later life showed that he had wide knowledge and a grasp of affairs. In 1885 he was instrumental in organizing the St. Louis local of musicians, in which he served as president and in other capacities until his death. Miller helped form the National League of Musicians; and he served as president of the organization during the 1891 term. He favored the affiliation of the NLM with the AFL and when the NLM refused to do so he was one of the musicians who helped organize the first convention of the American Federation of Musicians in 1896.

Owen Miller was active in labor affairs in the state of Missouri. He was a member of the State Senate of Missouri for a time and one of the leaders in the State Federation of Labor and in local councils. His opinions seemed to be highly respected in labor circles. It is clear that his advice was sought and accepted by the musicians, and that he wielded a cohesive influence upon the American Federation of Musicians during his lifetime. However, the achievements of his administration, which lasted until 1900, were negligible. Only the problem connected with matters of jurisdiction was solved. Some of the locals originally joining the Federation included on their membership rolls individuals expelled from other locals. This created a delicate situation. But the regulation of membership was turned over to the national union and an amicable adjustment was reached in individual cases.

In 1900, when nearly 49 years of age, Miller decided to step down from the presidency of the union. Although there had been some growth in the size of the organization, its progress had not been conspicuous. There were few signs to distinguish the AFM from its predecessor, the NLM. On the other hand, several of the very large and important Eastern locals had refused to join. The major factor which led to Miller's decision was financial. The salary of the president of the AFM was only $100 while that of the secretary was $750. Yet the burdens of the president's office were heavy. Miller therefore became secretary of the union and president of the St. Louis local. He added to his duties the editorship of the union's monthly magazine when it commenced publication in 1901. In this way his monetary income was increased. Joseph Nicholas Weber was elected to succeed Miller as president.

Unlike Miller, Weber was not a native of the United States. He was born in the Austro-Hungarian Empire on June 21, 1865,[7] and came to the United States when 14 years of age. He traveled widely in his capacity as a musician, playing the clarinet in various parts of the country. Weber joined the Denver musicians union in 1890 and soon demonstrated that he was politically able and adept. He became secretary of the Denver local and its delegate to the NLM. At the NLM convention of 1891 he favored affiliation with the AFL. In 1893 he joined the Seattle local and was elected vice president. In 1895, he went to Cincinnati, where his father, who was a bandleader, operated a saloon. The younger Weber was elected to the board of directors of the musicians union there. He then became president of the Cincinnati local and a delegate to the AFM convention. It is apparent that wherever he went, he soon emerged as one of the leaders of the local union. He was a conservative in his ideas and always clung to the view that changes should be made slowly but steadily.

Weber's first acts demonstrated that he was the actual and not merely nominal head of the organization. In short order, he crushed the smoldering resentment over his victory. Opposition was led by the editor of the *American Musician,* a monthly privately owned magazine. Under a contract with the AFM, this magazine served as the official publication of the musicians union. The editor, who previously had beaten Weber in an election held to select the delegate of the AFM to the AFL convention, was displeased with Weber's elevation, and he refused to take orders from Weber in regard to the contents of the magazine. The publication thereupon was suspended as the union periodical and the editor was expelled from the musicians union. During the next 40 years Weber was never again *seriously* challenged regarding his powers as head of the AFM.

Weber recognized that growth of the musicians union would take place only if the organization successfuly controlled competition in the industry. Musicians, much more than workers in most other occupations, have been mobile in seeking employment. Many of them have moved from town to town. If they were hindered from doing so by the rules of the labor union which solicited their membership, they did not join the organization but competed with it. Though the requirements for admission to the locals had been liberalized somewhat by 1900, the walls around each of them continued to exist. The AFM also faced the problem of competition from the traveling concert or military band. These bands sometimes lessened the employment opportunities of local musicians. Weber saw these problems and tried to solve them. He was fortunate in that circumstances arose which made it advisable for him to institute changes in the rules of the organization.

These circumstances developed in connection with the Chicago-Denver controversy of 1900. The AFM law at the time was that bands and orchestras were not permitted to accept engagements in the jurisdiction of a local other than their own without the consent of that other local. Violations subjected each offending member in the band or orchestra to a fine, half of which was paid to the national union and the remainder to the local where the infraction had occurred. This rule engendered much bitterness among the locals. Its most significant test occurred when a Chicago band performed an engagement in a Denver park without the consent of the Denver local. The Denver local fined the members of this band, but they refused to pay and the Chicago local refused to enforce the fine. As a result the Chicago local was expelled from the AFM. (It was later readmitted when it agreed to approve the fine.)

This incident forcefully brought to Weber's attention the fact that laws which created antagonisms between members or locals were not conducive to the furthering of the best interests of the Federation. It seemed at first that the only alternative to this severe restriction on the movement of musicians from place to place was a universal membership law which would make a member of one local automatically a member of all the other locals and entitle him to the rights and privileges of the members of the local in whose jurisdiction he was employed. Such membership rules, however, were not acceptable to the locals and could not be adopted.

A compromise was worked out which became known as the transfer law. Musicians were given the right to transfer from one jurisdiction to another, in order to seek employment. No obstacle to such movement could be set up by the local union in the area to which the musicians had migrated. Although this law has never been completely palatable to the locals and has caused much resentment over the years, it nevertheless was responsible more than any other factor for the rising fortunes of the union, which began to become apparent at that time. Members were permitted to move about, within the framework of the regulations of the union, and employers could hire union men who had come from other parts of the country. What formerly caused severe competition among musicians could be better controlled and regulated under the new policy. The AFM recognized the right of traveling members and traveling bands to operate within the union framework.

Many of the largest locals had refused to join the AFM because they feared that the opportunities of their members would be restricted if union musicians would be prohibited from traveling freely. (Most of the traveling shows that hired musicians and a large majority of the nation's leading instrumentalists were concentrated in the East.) The AFM therefore was forced to charter rival locals in several Eastern cities, though these unions typically remained of minor importance in their respective jurisdictions. Rival unionism was not at all unusual in the United States during this period, but the American Federation of Musicians energetically opposed all rivals. After passage of the transfer law Weber undertook to integrate and consolidate the musicians unions in the larger cities with renewed vigor. The situation was more propitious than previously because some of the fears and doubts of the larger independent locals had been allayed by the transfer law.

Though this law permitted all union members to come into the jurisdiction of the larger locals, it also entitled the members of the larger locals to go elsewhere. Furthermore, the larger locals recognized that the influx of competing musicians had been going on, anyhow. Now, at least, transfers were granted under the supervision of the AFM.

Over-all supervision by the national body was particularly helpful to a local like New York. Indeed, it would not have been possible for the New York local to unionize some of the theater houses, such as Loew, Fox, and Proctor, and the larger hotels, if it were not for the fact that the national union cooperated and kept potential strikebreakers from other locals out of New York City during the critical periods of negotiations. In 1904, Weber could appear before the ninth annual convention of the American Federation of Musicians and announce that amalgamations had been completed successfully during the preceding year in Philadelphia, Baltimore, Boston, Pittsburgh, and the important New York locals. The larger locals accepted the agreement which had been reached several years before on the method of voting at the convention. Larger locals were given a greater number of votes than smaller ones, but the maximum vote that could be cast by any local in a convention election was ten. This compromise restricted the power of the larger units and avoided one of the weaknesses of the NLM.

With the network of locals across the United States relatively complete, the national union was able to try to raise the economic status of musicians. Nonunion competition had to be reduced and union working conditions had to be established. The power of the contractors, who had often dominated the local to the disadvantage of the rank and file musicians, was reduced sharply. Band and orchestra conductors, in general, were required to become members of the union and as a result cooperation from them was obtained more readily. The union was always ready to bargain collectively with employers. It did not like to exert its economic strength by calling strikes. Said Weber: ". . . by far the most marked progress our organization has made was made by reason of its readiness to confer with the employer and settle controversies over the conference table."[8]

But even at the turn of the century the union was manifesting signs of unilateral action in fixing conditions of employment which have reappeared again and again throughout its history. When its power has enabled it to do so, this union has tended to lay down the law to employers without requesting their acquiescence and without consulting them. Back in 1904 a New York theater manager complained: "I notice that the union does not make any distinction between good and bad musicians. The bad ones, and they are many, get just as much pay as the good ones. Besides their regular pay they charge $2 extra for every holiday. There not being a sufficient number of legal holidays to suit them, they make holidays themselves. Easter Monday, St. Patrick's Day, and the eve's of New Year's, Washington's birthday, Thanksgiving and Christmas are all holidays in the eyes of musicians."[9]

Despite the resentment expressed by numerous employers, the union continued to flourish. Indeed, by 1905, the growing trade union of musicians had developed a position of more complete control over its business in the United States and Canada, to which it had extended its interests in 1900, than that occupied by any other union in the American Federation of Labor.[10] The achievement is outstanding when consideration is given to the status of workers and labor unions 50 years ago. At the turn of the century it was the general practice of management to oppose trade unionism and union men vigorously. Physical violence in labor relations during that period and the succeeding years was common. Discrimination against employees for union membership was not only lawful, but zealously pursued by employers. Yellow-dog contracts, blacklists, lockouts, and injunctions were regular weapons used against union members. It is a remarkable fact that under these conditions the union of musicians was able to secure complete control over the profession. For outside of employment on the railroads and in the building trades no other area of enterprise was strongly unionized. Moreover, on the railroads and in construction work, many distinct unions shared the membership.

A limited amount of dualism remained in the unionization of musicians in scattered sections of the country until the late 1930's, but the AFM was powerful enough to make the closed shop a characteristic of the working conditions of musicians in the United States. Quite early in its history, the AFM provided in its bylaws for the automatic expulsion of those members applying to the courts for injunctions. This rule helped the union prevent a weakening of the organization that could result from judicial intervention. The musicians union wholeheartedly accepted its leadership. The organizational success of the union at that early date enabled the leaders to turn their attention to the problems connected with nonunion competition and with increasing the employment opportunities of musicians.

"Owing to the rules of the Pressmen's Union of St. Louis,
Mo., the plant is compelled to employ a pressman all
the time, whether he is needed or not."

OWEN MILLER

• *The Changing Scene*

As the American Federation of Musicians grew, Weber's prestige increased too. The salary of $100 which he received in the
beginning was not particularly attractive but the power that went
with the position of president appealed to him. At first his
office was located in his home but in 1908 it was set up in separate quarters in New York. As the revenues derived by the AFM
increased, Weber was able to obtain a higher salary, furnish a
more luxurious office, and secure adequate clerical assistance.
His political sagacity was evidenced as he steered along a path
that was rife with factionalism. Weber was a politician of the
first order and he played his cards wisely. Because the union
was successful he received the benefit of every doubt from the
membership. Throughout his long tenure of office, however, he
was not able to escape bitter and severe censure from various
elements in the union. In 1912 Weber declared to the convention of the AFM that he would not run for re-election as president because of the general criticism expressed by the membership regarding his motives and his honesty. A petition signed by
every delegate to the convention induced him to alter his de-
termination.

The spells of sickness and the nervous breakdowns from which
Weber had always suffered, were becoming more acute. He reluctantly decided to step down from office in 1914 because of his
failing health and was designated president emeritus. Frank
Carothers was chosen president. Weber, however, could not resist the lure of activity and the power which he had yielded.
Without fanfare he was re-elected president of the AFM in 1915.

Immediately, his opponents renewed their campaign of persistently challenging his motives.

Although by the end of the first decade of the twentieth century, the AFM had settled the issues of artist versus worker, localism versus universality, and exclusion of membership versus expansion of membership, the first quarter of that century brought about many changes in the status of musicians and in the field of musical entertainment. Forms of musical rendition which were typical means of public diversion at the beginning of the period became obsolete or of minor importance as the years went on. The era was marked by the passing of the legitimate road show, the partial passing of burlesque, the decline in the use of music at picnics and excursions, the wane in the importance of the monster balls held by fraternal societies, and the adverse effects of prohibition on the employment opportunities of musicians. The epoch was also characterized by the disappearance of the traveling concert or military bands which had been the prime attractions in the amusement parks and theaters and which had been led by such outstanding conductors as John Philip Sousa, Arthur Pryor, Victor Herbert, and Giuseppe Creatore. These bands had utilized the services of hundreds of AFM members.

Other forms of musical diversion came to the fore. New types of music, known as ragtime, jazz, and swing became prominent. After a tenuous reception by the public, they became well established and popular. Though the employment opportunities of the older members were lessened because of their inability to adapt themselves satisfactorily, the AFM profited from the innovations. The traveling dance orchestra or name band had its origin about 1910 in connection with these developments. Previously performances by dance bands were rarely given beyond the neighboring areas and if played in territory adjacent to the home base, they were considered out-of-town engagements. The players returned home after every concert. Name bands, today, travel from place to place, and often do not return to their home base for many months. The popularity of the name band has continued to increase.

The AFM has been a highly complex organization, for it has had to deal with a diversity of employers. It has been required to negotiate with employers hiring musicians for operas, musical comedies, burlesques, motion pictures, symphony orchestras, vaudeville shows, concerts, dances, parades, and receptions. Some of this musical work may be considered to be permanent. The portion which represents only seasonal employment includes work in summer resorts and in municipal parks. The remainder is of a miscellaneous nature. In the midst of all these intricate and difficult relationships, the union was confronted with three major problems of competition. First, there was the question of the respective roles of the national union and the locals. The jurisdiction and powers of each had to be decided definitively. Secondly, the influx of foreign musicians, in so far as it served to undermine standards and curtail employment opportunities in the United States, had to be resisted. Thirdly, unfair competition from the bands organized by the armed forces had to be eliminated.

● *The Struggle with the New York Local*

During the 30-year period following the establishment of the American Federation of Musicians, the union was able to gain substantially improved working conditions from employers all over the United States; but, more important, the national organization conclusively was able to assert its hegemony over the local unions.

Some of the larger and more powerful locals had remained uncooperative and intractable after becoming affiliated with the American Federation of Musicians. Although the AFM slowly increased its membership and gradually was recognized as the spokesman of musicians by employers, it was not until the recalcitrance of the New York local was broken in the early 1920's that the domination of the national union was assured. Up to that time it was not clearly evident whether the national or the local would prevail in a test of strength between them.

When the AFM was organized in 1896 there were 16 distinct musicians unions in New York City but except for a few all of these were small and relatively unimportant. One of them, however, was the most important local union of musicians in the country. This local was the Musical Mutual Protective Union of New York, which had played a leading role in the NLM and which had fought against the establishment of the AFM. When the MMPU refused to affiliate, several minor unions in the city combined and formed local 7, AFM. Local 7 soon was expelled. The New York charter then was given to local 41, which immediately undertook to recruit the members of the MMPU. At first, the MMPU had 3,000 members and local 41 had 400 members but early in 1901, 1,000 members of the MMPU joined local 41. This group of a thousand, which belonged to both organizations, tried to bring the remaining Mutual musicians within the fold of the AFM.

The rivalry between these two New York locals was intense and for several years union musicians were incapable of dealing effectively with many employers because of the uncertainties associated with the divided jurisdiction and control. However, in July 1903 the MMPU and local 41 amalgamated. The new organization received a charter from the AFM, and was called local 310. The predominant element in the new local was the MMPU. The MMPU had been incorporated under the laws of New York State and therefore was entitled to a certain amount of freedom from interference in its internal affairs. Though the AFM requested local 310 to yield its state charter, this action was never taken by the local. The achievement of unity in New York City, however, was extremely important in furthering the establishment of control over employment opportunities by the musicians union.

Local 310 was an important unit of musicians. It included many of the country's leading instrumentalists and was cognizant of its prestige and strength. There was constant friction between this local and the national union because the local refused to subordinate its own interests to those of the AFM or of the other locals. The national was not anxious to bring about an open rupture or to provoke the local to secede so that frequently it did not press its prerogatives. Over the years, however, the prestige of the AFM suffered because the refractoriness of the local was known to employers and to the union's members.

The leadership of the New York local did not hide its antipathy to the national heads of the union and the local leaders felt pleased when they could set little obstacles in Weber's way. For many years Alexander Bremer was president of the New York local. He had been one of the most vitriolic opponents to the establishment of the AFM during the NLM days. In 1918, Bremer, then president of 310, was alleged to have expressed sympathy with the German cause. Upon the advice of Weber he was expelled from the local.[1] This incident showed that the New York local, despite its independence, nevertheless was subject to the influence of the national union. At the same time, it is known that Bremer's reported attitude in this matter was obnoxious to many of the members in his local.

In 1920, local 310 demanded an increase in the wages of musicians in the New York theaters. When the employers could not settle the matter with the local, they appealed to the national union to adjust the dispute so that a strike would be averted. Weber entered the negotiations and reached an agreement with the employers. His action, however, crystallized resentment against the AFM among New York musicians. Several hundred members in the local were dissatisfied with the arbitrary way in which the national officers had stepped in, and disapproved the terms of the settlement. This faction formed a club within the local known as the "Quorum Club," ostensibly to guarantee the presence of a quorum at every membership meeting of the union, but actually to gain and maintain control of local 310. At the next election it succeeded in gaining a majority on the board of directors of the local by concentrating its votes on a few candidates, but it was unsuccessful in an attempt to win the presidency.

The president of the local soon was in conflict with his board of directors and when he acted in violation of the rules of the local, the board suspended him from office. He appealed to Weber and Weber set aside the action of the board. But the members of the board disregarded Weber's order and ejected the president from a subsequent meeting. As a result, they were expelled from the union. Since such action, if enforced, would mean the loss of employment to the directors, they appealed to the courts to set aside Weber's expulsion order. The decision handed down by a New York court was that Weber had no right to interfere in the internal affairs of local 310 because it was incorporated under the laws of the state. The court said: "If the union itself [local 310] had committed any act which was repugnant to the purposes of the federation, the right of affiliation might have been withdrawn."[2]

The members of the board of directors of local 310 became bolder after their reinstatement by order of the New York Supreme Court. They decided not to receive transfer cards deposited by members of other locals. This action, however, violated the bylaws of the American Federation of Musicians. Local 310 was given a hearing and then suspended by the national executive board early in July 1921.

Plans were made by local 310 to organize a rival national union, but they never materialized. The strike which the local called in the New York theaters was unsuccessful and the union suffered a serious defeat. Employment conditions in New York were becoming demoralized. New York theater owners had to decide whether to deal with the AFM or with the New York local. By a narrow margin they agreed to negotiate with Weber and the national union. This move by the employers decided the issue and spelled the defeat of the Musical Mutual Protective Union.

When the possibility of a rapid influx of musicians from all over the country became likely during the period in which no unit of musicians recognized by the national union functioned in New York City, some of the instrumentalists acted quickly to forestall chaotic conditions. They presented a petition from more than a thousand musicians in the city and requested the AFM to charter a new local. The national union agreed to do so but only after the petitioners stipulated that the officers of the new local were to be appointed by the national union and that the rules and regulations of the local would be subject to the approval of the AFM executive board. Local 802 in New York City was then chartered on August 27, 1921.

Before long almost all of the members of the MMPU had joined local 802. Though the MMPU never had more than 8,000 members, local 802 encompassed 12,000 musicians shortly after being formed. The increase came about mainly because of the nominal initiation fee of two dollars which had been set. Musicians who had refused to join when the entrance fee was high hastened to take advantage of this opportunity. Local 802 took over control of the labor relations of musicians in the city. Most of the members of the MMPU continued to maintain their connection with that organization because the MMPU owned property (mainly, a building) valued in excess of a half million dollars.

A few of the ringleaders in the Quorum Club were not permitted to join local 802 and these disgruntled members applied to the courts for an order to reinstate local 310 in the AFM and to dissolve local 802. The New York courts, however, were not hospitable to the contentions of the plaintiffs and ruled that the AFM had acted in accordance with its rights.[3] Nevertheless court litigation of this issue cost the AFM and local 802 the sum of $250,000. At the height of the struggle Weber had to be protected by city detectives but eventually the unions became reconciled. The Musical Mutual Protective Union changed its name to the Mutual Musical Corporation and for several years leased the building which it owned, to local 802. The Mutual Musical Corporation was dissolved in 1947 and its property was divided among 900 persons—600 members and 300 heirs of members.

The events in the dispute between the American Federation of Musicians and the New York local had reverberated throughout the organization but their aftermath was beneficial to the national union. It was established decisively that local rules were valid only if they did not conflict with those of the AFM. Since then, the organization has been much more cohesive and the authority of the national officers has been more apparent. Weber had won one of the major victories of his career.

● *Competition from Foreign Musicians*

Establishment of the principle of national supremacy over the local was an internal matter within the scope of union politics. Much more difficult were the attempts to regulate the importation of foreign musicians and to prevent the competition of military and naval bands. The existence of these conditions tended to negate the organizational efforts of the union and made it more difficult for the AFM to establish control over the musical industries.

The musicians union was anxious to enlist all American instrumental players within its organization. But there was no desire to increase the number of musicians unduly. The device of restricting the number of workers available for employment in specific occupations and thereby enabling such workers to gain more concessions from employers was well known to labor unions and practiced by many of them. Traditionally, the American Federation of Labor has opposed immigration, for the immigrant has been considered as a source of competition to the laborer in the United States. The musicians gave their complete support to this notion, and they favored a governmental policy which would impose very limited immigration quotas.

The half century preceding 1910 was one in which millions of persons were entering the country. The American people, in general, did not desire to cut off this influx, for the spirit of boundless economic opportunity was still characteristic of the times. Labor, however, turned its attention to those groups of immigrants which were a direct and immediate threat to labor standards. Unlike Europe where the abundance of labor has tended to depress wages, wage rates in the United States, as in other new countries where workers have been relatively scarce, always have been comparatively high. These higher wage rates have attracted the foreigner to American shores.

It was not too difficult for unscrupulous individuals to undermine American wages, hours, and working conditions, and at the same time benefit personally, by deliberately importing aliens, on a contractual basis, to work for wages lower than those to which workers in the United States were accustomed. Such activities were possible because of the marked disparity between American and European wages. Recognizing the harmful effects emanating from these circumstances, in 1885 Congress passed a law forbidding an individual from importing and contracting with aliens to perform labor in the United States. In 1907, a proviso was added that skilled and unskilled contract laborers were not to be admitted to this country. The labor movement was solidly behind the alien contract labor legislation. The musicians were in full agreement with these laws but nevertheless they did not benefit from them, because the Attorney General ruled that musicians were not included within the scope of the enactments. Musicians, he declared, were artists and professionals, not laborers. Under the legislation, contracts could be entered into for the purpose of importing alien artists.

Though the musicians union did endeavor for many years to bring about a reversal in the pronouncement of the Attorney General, it also undertook to use its own economic pressures to combat the entry of foreign musicians. It refused to stand by idly while hundreds of musicians were brought in from various parts of Europe under contract. Members of the American

Federation of Musicians involved in bringing over alien instrumentalists were subject to fines and other penalties. Agents and employers of the imported individuals were put on an unfair list, and union members were barred from working for them. Contract labor musicians were excluded from membership in the union; under the rules only citizens or those who had secured first papers were eligible to join.

It was in connection with this issue that Walter Damrosch was fined by the union in 1905. Damrosch came to this country in 1871, at the age of nine. Soon, because of his musical talent, he had achieved a reputation as an eminent conductor. He joined the MMPU of New York, but when he attempted to hire a nonunion violoncellist in 1893, he was nearly expelled from the union. The matter, however, was adjusted.[4] In 1903, Damrosch became director of the New York Symphony Orchestra and undertook to reorganize it. The wood-wind section was particularly weak, and feeling that the musicians best-able to play those instruments were to be found in France, Damrosch went there and brought back five players. It was his contention that New York musicians were unsatisfactory performers on wood winds and that better players were necessary to enable the New York orchestra to compete successfully with the nonunion Boston Symphony Orchestra. The other members of the New York orchestra were all in the union and they refused to play with the five Frenchmen. The New York local then decided that the five could play only as "soloists," since, at that time, under such circumstances they were not required to be union members.

Public opinion and the New York press were behind Damrosch and excoriated the musicians union, but the French instrumentalists could not play. Damrosch appealed to the national officers in 1905, and they were more amenable to his arguments and the public pressure. The men were permitted to enroll in the New York local and play with the orchestra. But for violating the laws of the AFM in bringing over alien musicians, Damrosch was fined a thousand dollars. Damrosch paid the fine.[5]

The union was highly critical of foreign bands which were brought to this country by agents and employers. The union strongly opposed the entry of Giuseppe Creatore and his band of 55 men from Italy in 1902. Several years later, Creatore unsuccessfully tried to take the Italian musicians out of the Philadelphia local of the AFM.[6] The American Federation of Musicians fought a plethora of imported Royal Italian bands which seemed to be playing everywhere.

The Federation of Musicians also tried to bring to an end the productions of the French Opera Company of New Orleans. This company contracted for the services of foreign musicians and paid their transportation costs to the United States. The musicians were paid wages far below the union scale. They played three months in New Orleans and three months on the road, after which they were free to drift. If they returned to Europe, they had to pay their own costs of transportation. If they remained in the United States, they were ineligible to join the AFM since under the rules of the union, contract labor musicians could not be accepted. Some of these men continued to play for the company in succeeding seasons. The AFM itself occasionally undertook to finance these musicians back to Europe, in order to get rid of them. The union declared that it was willing to admit a musician who came to this country of his own volition and with an intent to find employment by his own efforts, but that it would not admit alien contract musicians, unless the circumstances were exceptional. In 1908, with the aid of President Theodore Roosevelt, the union was able to prevent importation of musicians by the Metropolitan Opera House.[7] Except in Boston, the AFM was strong enough to prevent the symphony orchestras from bringing in foreign musicians.

The secretary of the AFM wrote constantly to the musicians unions in France, England, and other European countries warning them of the difficulties of obtaining employment in the United States and of the high cost of living here. The foreign unions seemed to appreciate the problem of competitive wages and always promised their cooperation. As the years passed, competition from foreign bands gradually became negligible. A Congressional law in 1917 re-enacted the ban on the immigration of contract laborers, and this statute was interpreted by the Secretary of Labor, through the Bureau of Immigration, to include ordinary musicians. Only instrumental soloists were admitted under the provision permitting the entry, under contract, of artists.

Nevertheless in spite of favorable Congressional action, court decisions modified the intent of the legislation of 1917. The meaning of artist was gradually expanded, so that many bands and orchestras were admitted to this country under that designation. Finally, an amendment was passed in 1932, which specifically prohibits the entry of alien instrumental musicians under the category of artist, unless they show distinguished merit and ability.[8] The long battle of the AFM was ended. No further importation of alien musicians has taken place. Problems with regard to refugee musicians which arose in the early 1940's were quite different, because the refugees entered under a quota, had no employment contract in advance, and were eligible to join the union.

Ironically, the contract labor laws were applied by the United States to prevent the movement of musicians from Canada into this country. The AFM, which had many members in Canada, did not especially desire to block their entry into the United States but could not induce the authorities to permit Canadian contract musicians to enter. The Canadian government, on the other hand, at first did not bar contract labor musicians from admission. An order in council in 1929, however, prohibited labor under contract, in general, from entering Canada. This was interpreted by Canadian immigration authorities to mean that, with the exception of concert groups and outstanding soloists, foreign musicians could enter Canada under contract only if the same number of Canadian musicians were employed on the same engagement and for the same hours. After the second World War the general order was suspended because of the need for skilled workers.[9] This action caused a movement of traveling cocktail and tavern groups of musicians into Canada; though similar privileges were not available to Canadian instrumentalists. Leaders of the AFM have been attempting to get the governments of the United States and Canada to work out a reciprocal arrangement in connection with this problem.

On the domestic scene the hostility of the union to a practice similar to contract labor was manifested by its fight against colonization. Although the union adopted the transfer law which permitted the free movement of musicians from jurisdiction to jurisdiction in seeking employment, union rules did not permit an employer to bring in single musicians from other locals nor for an individual member who intended to go to an area under the jurisdiction of another local to contract with an employer for a job in advance of his arrival. This practice was known as colonizing and was outlawed by the AFM. One of the contentions of local 310 at the time of its expulsion was that it refused to accept the transfer cards of members seeking admittance to the territory within its jurisdiction because those members were colonizers. The ban did not apply to traveling dance bands.

● *Competition from the Army and the Navy*

Elimination of the competition of other musicians was the main task of the AFM during the first two and a half decades of this century. For in addition to the competition of contract aliens the union was faced with the pressing issue of competition from groups within the country. Rival unionism never was a serious problem to the musicians union. Although nonunion competition from unorganized workers and from bands of children, amateurs, fraternal orders, and institutions were more important, even these activities were not significant. But competition from musicians employed by the federal government gave rise to the most widely publicized grievance of the union during this period. This issue related almost entirely to the bands of the army and navy, although occasionally other units were involved. In 1915, for example, the Letter Carriers Band of Omaha received a city contract to play in the public parks because it had accepted a wage scale lower than the one indicated in the union bid; and the resulting dispute with city officials and the Postmaster General was settled only with great difficulty.

The union cannot perform its economic functions of improving the wages, hours, and working conditions of its members effectively, if it is unable to prevent undercutting of its price schedules. Elimination of this practice required the union to be in a position where it could exercise disciplinary control over the musicians who played for a price under the wage scale. The musician in the armed forces acted in the role of undercutter. But these men have not been permitted to join or remain active members of the American Federation of Musicians since the union has not been in a position to exercise control over their actions.

Historically, the musician enlisting in the army was allowed to take outside engagements providing the engagements did not interfere with his other duties—which involved playing at guard mount, rehearsal, dress parade, and evening concert. This schedule, however, actually made it impossible for the enlisted musician to compete seriously with the civilian. But since the rate of pay was low a sufficient number of competent musicians did not enlist in the services; despite the relatively greater economic security which these men would have had if they had done so. The Secretary of War in James Madison's cabinet, as an inducement to attract musicians, permitted commanding officers to grant regular "leaves of absence" to the band. This action made possible the acceptance of other opportunities of employment. Civilian musicians filed protests with the War Department against such competition as early as 1824, but these protests were unheeded.

It was not until 1885, that the War Department issued an order, which was reinforced by a circular letter in 1897, prohibiting army bands from engaging to play at prices disproportionately lower than those of other bands performing similar services. This order seemed to meet the most serious objections of the local unions, except that in the course of the next 30 years, hundreds of cases were tabulated by the NLM and AFM in which the order was violated.

The first convention of the National League of Musicians, which met in March 1886, passed a resolution protesting against army competition; later that year General Philip Sheridan, who was in charge of the United States Army, ordered the confinement of army bands to their military duties. Immediately thereafter, however, the Secretary of War abrogated this order. Under the renewed pressure of the musicians, the Secretary ordered that the military bands stationed at the recruiting depots of the army (St. Louis, Missouri; Columbus, Ohio; and Governor's Island, New York) had to remain at their reservations except by special permission. But the competition of all other army bands and of all naval bands persisted. The succeeding Secretaries of War ignored the confinement order, and the limited concession to civilian musicians thus became a dead letter.

The musicians took their case directly to President Theodore Roosevelt at the White House late in 1903 and he promised some redress, but the competition from military bands continued. The AFM convention of 1903, however, already had passed a resolution that no union musician was permitted to play at any function where a government service band also was employed or engaged. This resolution was partially successful in achieving its objective and was of great benefit to the AFM until the passage of legislation in 1908, and even thereafter.

Lack of cooperation from the executive branch of the government led the musicians to turn their attention to Congress. Some attempts were made by Congressmen in the 1880's to obtain passage of bills barring enlisted musicians from competing with civilians. At first, these efforts were unavailing. Finally in 1908, with the aid of Congressman Richard Bartholdt, a Republican member of the House, the musicians obtained what they had desired. Congress included provisions in both the army and navy appropriations bills forbidding army and navy musicians from competing with civilians. The pay of army musicians was increased and navy musicians received the benefit of a general increase to enlisted naval personnel.

These bills were approved in the middle of May. At the end of May, the Secretary of the Navy requested an opinion from the Attorney General, as to whether the Act applied to the United States Marine Band. In November, after a delay of more than five months, the Attorney General, Charles J. Bonaparte, replied that the Marine Band was exempt from the provision barring competition from naval bands, since it was not a naval band.[10]

The union fought the exemption of the United States Marine Band and the violations of the law committed by army and navy bands. For many years complaints against the infractions of the 1908 provisions were made to the appropriate administrative officials, though generally without avail. In 1916, Democratic Senator James A. Reed succeeded in attaching an amendment to a bill increasing the size of the army. The amendment prohibited enlisted musicians of the army, navy, and marines from engaging in any task which would conflict with the opportunities of civilian musicians. The bill became law in 1916.[11]

This law was enforced strictly under the administration of President Wilson. Beginning with the inauguration of President Harding, competition from naval bands again developed, although the union did not complain of any army infractions. At Weber's request, Samuel Gompers, president of the AFL, protested the Navy's interpretation of the law to President Coolidge in 1924. But Coolidge's noncommittal reply was that he would favor remedial legislation. It was not until 1934 that the Navy ended the practice of allowing its bands to compete with civilian musicians. The American Federation of Musicians has not objected to the use of enlisted bands for military purposes and on military occasions or in patriotic and charitable activities which are national in scope and nonpartisan and nonsectarian in character. In the last 10 years, local and isolated cases of competition from bands of the armed forces have occurred and the AFM only recently has succeeded in getting the matter adjusted at the higher levels.

During the first World War the AFM put forth efforts to improve the status of the military bandsmen. The union favored a program under which musicians would serve in a capacity where their musical talent would be utilized, the size of the band would be enlarged, and bandleaders would be raised to commissioned rank. Sometimes, an army bandleader was not even a noncommissioned officer. Near the end of the war, General John J. Pershing ordered that United States army bands in France should be increased from 28 to 50 men and that the leader of the band should be raised to the rank of first or second lieutenant depending upon the length of his army experience as bandleader.

The strength of the union enabled it to force a gradual, but substantial, upward movement in wage rates during the second decade of the twentieth century. The main countermove on the part of employers was to reduce the number of musicians they employed. The problem of unemployment which emerged both from this action of employers and from the growing membership of the union was solved by the advent of the war. Many members of the musicians union in the United States and Canada enlisted or were drafted into the armed forces. This process reduced the number of available civilian musicians and brought about a better balance between the demand for and the supply of musical services.

The American Federation of Musicians had developed from a puny organization in 1896 to one whose power and prestige were unrivaled in the labor movement by 1925. It exercised unquestioned and complete control over its internal affairs after the New York local was subdued. And by that time, with the aid of

Congressional alien contract labor laws and restrictions on military and naval bands, it largely had eliminated competition from musicians who were not members of the union. But though it tightened its restrictions on employers, it complained of certain union practices which affected its own printing plant. Plaintively Owen Miller reported to the AFM convention: "Owing to the rules of the Pressmen's Union of St. Louis, Mo., the plant is compelled to employ a pressman all the time, whether he is needed or not."[12] This was a practice which locals of the AFM themselves subsequently adopted.

Nevertheless, the musicians' chief problem from a competitive force was yet to arise. It developed from various technological advances.

"... Petrillo ... is, to my almost certain knowledge and
to my strong conviction, not a crook."

WESTBROOK PEGLER

Petrillo's Early Life

"... Petrillo ... is, to my almost certain knowledge and to my
strong conviction, not a crook."[1] Westbrook Pegler, who does not
generally think highly of labor leaders, condescended to make
this statement about Petrillo. Even though it is expressed in
negative terms, it may be assumed that Pegler made a relatively
exhaustive inquiry into the most unfavorable aspects of Petrillo's
life. Yet Petrillo met Pegler's test of honesty. Who is Petrillo?
Where does he come from? How did he get his power? What
does he do with it? The answer to these questions will go far
towards explaining the attitude and position of the American
Federation of Musicians today on many issues.

James Caesar Petrillo was born in Chicago on March 16, 1892,
and spent almost all of his first 50 years in that city. He was
raised in an environment dominated by misery and violence but
he seemed to thrive under those conditions. Early in his life,
Petrillo became connected with the work of the labor movement
in the field of music; and with the prevalence of gangsterism and
hoodlumism in the Chicago area for many years, he found that
a person had to be tough in order to get ahead in union politics.
James C. Petrillo, whose youthful experiences with strong-arm
methods and tactics proved to be of great value to him, was of
that mold. He has maintained a fondness for such rough actions
to this day, even though he no longer has to employ them.

In order to understand Petrillo, it is necessary to depict the
conditions prevailing among the musicians in Chicago. A Chicago
Musical Union was formed in 1857, but it disbanded in 1865
because of the competition of other fraternal societies and because

of the demands of business interests on the time of its members. It is doubtful whether the purposes of this organization were similar to those characterizing a trade union today. A local of musicians was established in 1864 but it remained in existence only a decade. The first permanent union in Chicago was organized in 1880. Soon several rival unions of musicians were in existence though none showed any substantial growth. When the AFM was established, one of the locals in Chicago, which had about 750 members, received the charter numbered 10. But it withdrew from the AFM in 1898 and was replaced almost immediately by an amalgamated unit of several locals—the Chicago Federation of Musicians—which then totaled 1,400 members. The details of the Chicago-Denver controversy of 1900 and the expulsion and readmission of local 10 already have been narrated. The union charter thus dates from 1901. The following year a local of Negro musicians was chartered in Chicago as number 208. Local 208 never has been completely independent, since it has had to abide by some of the rules of the white local.

From 1900 to 1937, the most prominent case of dual unionism among musicians in the United States was found in Chicago. The American Musicians Union, which attempted to establish a national labor union, had its strongest base there, and for a time its membership was as large as that of the Chicago local of the AFM. These two unions struggled bitterly with each other to control employment in that city. Generally, local 10 was more successful because of the advantage which it derived from its affiliation with the AFM. The AFM could bring pressure to bear on the employer, if the employer had other business connections in the field of music outside of Chicago. The American Musicians Union tried to get the courts to force members of the AFM to work with its own members, but it was not successful.

As the membership of the Chicago Federation of Musicians expanded, it became necessary for the local to obtain larger and more adequate quarters. The Chicago Musicians Club therefore was incorporated to acquire property. The union soon was able to acquire a building for $75,000 on a 99-year lease. Membership in the Club was limited to persons already in local 10 and provided a social link among the musicians. In 1933, during

Petrillo's regime, the local moved into a new two-story building which cost over a hundred thousand dollars to construct and which was paid for in cash.

Petrillo's father, who came to this country from Italy and settled in Chicago, worked for the city as a sewer digger. He raised a family of five children. His only other son, Caesar James, is a dance band conductor and trombone player for CBS. James Caesar was not a bright boy. Although he attended the Dante Elementary School for nine years, he never got beyond the fourth grade. "They bounced me around," he complained. "One year I would be in the fourth grade and next year in the third. They drove me nuts! After nine years I give it up."[2] It is not unexpected, therefore, that he never gained a good command of the English language, although he has shown improvement over the years. Profanity and blasphemy are liberally interspersed in his conversation and he uses adjectives only on formal occasions.

When Jimmy was eight years old his father bought him a trumpet, but despite much practice he never learned to play it well. For eight years he played on the Chicago Daily News band. He also played a trumpet in the Hull House band where he received free music lessons. But he was an ambitious boy. He sold newspapers, ran elevators, drove a delivery cart, and sold peanuts and papers on the railroads. Later he opened a cigar stand and he helped to run a saloon. Petrillo showed courage and pugnacity. He did not avoid fights, and it is reported that he once beat nine boys, one at a time, in two hours of continuous fighting. Petrillo formerly took part in the annual Chicago affair in which executives who were sometime newsboys, sold newspapers on the streets for one day in order to bolster a Christmas fund.

At 14 he organized his own four-piece dance band and although he was under the minimum age limit, was permitted to join the American Musicians Union by special dispensation. He played at dances, at weddings, at picnics, in beer gardens, and on band wagons. It was not uncommon for some of these engagements to break up in fights. This represented a typical example of existence for many Chicago musicians.

Before long, Petrillo "lost his lip" and switched to politics. Though he also had tried to play the drum, he never had learned to do so well. He was more successful in his political endeavors within the union. After several years, he had established himself as a powerful figure in the AMU. In 1914 he was elected president of the union at the age of 22. He served in that office for three years with mediocre success and then was defeated for re-election. Petrillo was so disappointed by the defeat that he resigned from the American Musicians Union and early in 1918 joined the Chicago local of the AFM.

● *Petrillo in the Chicago Local*

The political activity within the local was his main interest and he was assigned the task of organizing the musicians in the Chinese restaurants. The task was difficult since Chicago was torn by labor wars and racketeering. But Petrillo already was accustomed to rough tactics. His methods were not tactful but they were very effective and in a short time he unionized most of those restaurants. As a result he was elected vice president in 1919.

The Chicago theater strike at the end of 1920 was marked by much intimidation and many threats of violence. The local was torn by internal strife and dissension. One faction was responsible for assaulting and inflicting a severe beating on the president of local 10, Joseph F. Winkler, early in 1922,[3] for exploding a bomb in the offices of the union, and for blackmailing the board of directors. It was during this period of internecine difficulty that Petrillo was elected president of the local. The year was 1922.

One of the first important actions undertaken by the new president was to require radio stations to pay musicians. Previously musicians had played over the airwaves merely for the advantages which such publicity gave them. Petrillo described his negotiations with the stations: "They told me to see their lawyer. The lawyer was usually an ex-Judge So-and-So. He had a lot of books on the table to prove the Government owned the air. I said, 'I know the Government owns the air. What I want to find out is who pays the musicians!' We won the fight."[4] In 1924 the porch of Petrillo's home was wrecked and the windows blown out by a bomb.

In 1927, the Chicago local went out on strike against the theaters in what represented the biggest walkout in the history of the AFM. An attempt to secure an injunction restraining Petrillo was blocked in the federal courts by his lawyers, Clarence Darrow, Donald Richberg, and David Lilienthal. The union gained its demands after four days. Under threat of a strike, Petrillo also was able to complete the task of unionizing the hotels in 1931. He won wage increases from the restaurants, theaters, opera, and symphony. He negotiated the first musicians' contract with a radio station when he signed with WMAQ.

Chicago's most important jobs for musicians soon were controlled by Petrillo. Although there was a rival union and many nonunionists in the city, the Chicago Federation of Musicians gradually gained more control. Scores of conductors of dance bands joined the union after being subjected to strong pressure. Petrillo had to clash with many notables in order to protect the interests of the musicians. When Charles G. Dawes was Vice President of the United States, during the second term of the administration of Calvin Coolidge, he was touring through Europe and became interested in some Hungarian musicians. The La Salle Hotel imported them for an engagement on Dawes' recommendation. Petrillo was furious. "Where do those foreigners get off coming in here when my boys are walking the streets? Who does Dawes think he is?"[5] Petrillo threatened to cut off the hotel from the radio and from the services of his musicians but he relented and permitted the Hungarian musicians to stay for six months when the hotel agreed to hire members of local 10 for all functions held in the hotel. This dispute apparently left no hard feelings between Petrillo and Dawes because in 1929, Dawes made a contribution of $1,000 to support a series of outdoor band concerts sponsored by the Chicago musicians union.

Petrillo also tangled with Benito Mussolini. The sponsors of an Italian jubilee scheduled for Chicago in 1931 arranged to have a nonunion band. Petrillo cabled Mussolini that his consul in Chicago had failed to cooperate with the union. The response which he received was not favorable, although an Italian band and a union band both played at the jubilee. During the same year Chicago elected Anton J. Cermak as mayor. Cermak planned to use a high school band at his inauguration ceremonial. This meant that professional musicians would not be employed. But as the new mayor also was to broadcast over the NBC network, Petrillo warned the radio station that he would call a strike if it allowed that broadcast to take place. The high school band was withdrawn and a band of 50 musicians from local 10 led the inaugural procession.

Late in 1931, Petrillo was held up and robbed of $1,900 as he was returning home one night. As a result he increased the number of bodyguards which surrounded him. Later, the city of Chicago assigned two detectives to stay with him while he was in the city. Chicago continued to give him this special protection until the end of 1945. When he traveled at night he had a half-dozen men with him. For a time he rode in a bulletproof car and had bulletproof windows in his office. Reporters found bullet marks on the rear window of his car when he traded it in for a new one in 1936. Towards the end of 1933 there were rumors that Petrillo had been kidnaped by the Touhy mob in June, and had been ransomed by the union for $100,000. Two members of the local filed a suit to secure an accounting of the funds of the local four days before the union election in December.[6] In the few days that remained, Petrillo had accountants audit the books of the local and certify that they were in perfect order. Then he spent several thousand dollars to notify the membership of the result and to advertise in the newspapers. His two opponents were defeated decisively in the election for the presidency and the suit filed against him was thrown out of court for want of prosecution. One of Petrillo's opponents for the presidency suddenly lost the job he had held in a theater. He was not able to find another position for several years and when he did it was in another state. Since the balloting in 1933 Petrillo has been unopposed in local elections.

James Caesar Petrillo lived a hectic life during the depression years, but the local prospered. Union affairs involved him in many difficult problems and required numerous decisions, but he met and made them all. Petrillo was concerned with the economic opportunities of musicians at a time when unemployment was high and when very few musicians had full-time jobs in their profession. Although Chicago had employed about 2,000 musicians in its theaters before the coming of the sound films, by the mid-1930's only 125 jobs remained. In order to increase employment, Petrillo tried to get the city of Chicago to give free summer concerts in the public parks, but he was unsuccessful. He therefore decided to get on one of the park boards. Governor Henry Horner of Illinois appointed Petrillo to the West Park Board in 1933, upon the recommendation of Mayor Cermak. After Chicago's park boards were merged, Petrillo was put on the new board by his friend, Mayor Edward J. Kelly.

The park board however refused to appropriate any money for concerts. The Chicago local, in presenting free concerts, spent many thousands of dollars in 1935 to pay musicians. Millions of persons attended those highly successful concerts. The city reconsidered its opposition and then decided to subsidize them. The union continued to bear part of the cost and until 1943, it paid the soloists. Much employment has been provided by this project.

Petrillo has supported the Democratic party in politics. The Chicago local made a substantial contribution to Roosevelt's campaign in 1936 and then welcomed the President with a 300-piece band when he came to that city. In 1939, Petrillo celebrated Mayor Kelly's re-election in an affair at the Chicago stadium by "requesting" the appearance of 19 of the country's leading name bands and four leading symphony orchestras. When, however, Chicago politicians of the Republican and Democratic parties had tried to play recorded music from sound trucks during the election campaign of 1932, Petrillo threatened to force them off the radio. Music for political rallies in Chicago now is provided by live musicians.

As Petrillo tightened his control over the affairs of the musicians of Chicago, he began reaching out on a wider scale. At the 1927 convention of the AFM he was defeated for election as a member of the international executive board, running fifth in a field of five. Four years later Petrillo, who already had received the praise of Weber for his conduct during the Chicago theater negotiations, was defeated by Charles L. Bagley for the vice presidency of the national union, in the race to choose a successor to William L. Mayer. Bagley is still the union's vice president. However, in 1932 Petrillo was elected to the executive board and his power on a national scale began to grow.

● *Petrillo at Odds with John L. Lewis*

A serious challenge was presented to the musicians of Chicago by the organization of the CIO. John L. Lewis, of the United Mine Workers, who headed the CIO, was searching for a union of musicians which would affiliate with the CIO. In 1937 he invited the American Musicians Union, which comprised 2,500 members in Chicago, to join his federation as the nucleus of a new national organization. Petrillo acted quickly. He temporarily waived the initiation fee of the Chicago local, which was $100 for new members, and almost all the musicians in the AMU joined his organization. On this occasion the Chicago Federation of Musicians also absorbed the Polish-American Musicians Union. These developments marked the end of any competitive threat which had faced the AFM from rival unionism. Subsequent attempts by the CIO to organize musicians were failures.

The clash between Lewis and Petrillo had begun in 1936. William Green, president of the AFL, was a member of the United Mine Workers. In 1936, when the AFL suspended the CIO unions, one of which was the Mine Workers, it appeared as if Green would hold no membership in any AFL union. Petrillo came to his aid and made him a member of the musicians union. During 1944, however, Green expressed his opposition to a series of Midwestern strikes by the AFM against the broadcasters because labor had given its pledge not to strike during the war. On that occasion, Petrillo attacked Green for failing to clean out racketeering in the AFL and told him to keep out of the internal affairs of the musicians union.

One rash act committed by Petrillo was corrected by the pressure of public opinion. Late in 1939, Petrillo ordered the theaters to eliminate all mention of the name of John L. Lewis from two plays being performed in Chicago theaters. In George White's *Scandals,* Lewis was named in a skit performed by Willie Howard; and Lewis also was referred to in several lines of *The Man Who Came to Dinner.* The theaters complied but the country's press attacked Petrillo. Critics called him a censor. A national issue was avoided only when Petrillo hastily withdrew his order and the lines were restored in the two plays. He recalls: "They said I was un-Constitutional and all that stuff. I never had nothing like that in my mind.[7]. . . I just thought I'd push Lewis around a little."[8]

In June 1949, Petrillo renewed his quarrel with Lewis. In an address to the delegates of the AFM convention, Petrillo criticized Lewis for ordering the miners not to work during the period when Congress was considering labor legislation. He said: "So far as I'm concerned—and I invite the press to record this— I think John L. Lewis is nuts. I say to him: 'You are not a faithful labor leader, nor are you faithful to the people of America.' There it is. Somebody had to say it, so I did. I have a right to say it—I'm a sincere labor leader. . . . I'll take him on here—on the radio—any place in America."[9] Later that month, Petrillo sent telegrams to several United States Senators and other high government officials criticizing the intransigent position of Lewis in regard to the repeal of the Taft-Hartley law.[10]

● *The Situation in Chicago*

The Chicago Federation of Musicians has grown and prospered under Petrillo's leadership. For many years it was the second largest local of musicians in the United States and only recently it has fallen to third rank, but it remains the most powerful and aggressive local in establishing and maintaining employment opportunities in its jurisdiction. Petrillo pioneered in developing the standby in the field of music. (A standby is a musician who is engaged to be present on a certain occasion though he is not expected to render any services.) The practice has been utilized by the union especially when the employer desired to use a nonunion musician, but it also has been used when the employer has hired a union musician from another jurisdiction. Sometimes a standby fee has been paid to the union but no musicians have been required to appear for work.

Close scrutiny by Congress of various practices by the musicians union has made the AFM less inclined to use the standby. Standbys have been eliminated completely from the radio by the Lea Act of 1946. Formerly Petrillo frequently utilized this device whenever amateurs or children were employed as musical performers. Petrillo also succeeded in adopting a related make-work scheme. Employers, particularly in the theaters, are required to hire a minimum number of men for an engagement. There is little doubt that on many occasions fewer musicians would suffice for the purposes of the producers. He has eliminated free rehearsals and he has banned the practice whereby musicians have played without pay in a public place for their own amusement on occasions when other musicians might have been hired. When Alec Templeton and Tommy Dorsey played some music while waiting for studio pictures to be taken after a broadcast, Petrillo sent the advertising agency which handled the show a bill for $33 overtime.

Petrillo is a tough man to deal with. Formerly, he accepted a compromise only as a last resort; though frequently his opening demands during negotiations merely are maneuvers to secure a more strategic bargaining position. His word is good and all employers who have dealt with him admit readily that his oral promise is just as satisfactory as a written contract. Nor has he ever violated or broken contracts. Petrillo does not tolerate performers who are not doing their best, or who appear late or who get to work in an inebriated condition. These players are warned and fined, if the circumstances warrant such action. The policy of the AFM has never been to guarantee jobs to specific musicians. Each man stands or falls on his own merit.

At the head of the Chicago local stands the president with wide discretionary powers. There are six other members on the board of directors elected by the musicians. This board acts on all matters not specifically provided for in the bylaws. The union has a trial board of nine men, a body of original jurisdiction, which hears all charges of violations of wage scales and union bylaws. This board is elected by the members and like the other officials has a five-year term. The president may appoint a group of assistants to aid him in conducting the affairs of the local.[11]

The revenues of the local are derived from initiation fees of $50, annual dues of $16 or $20, and an income tax on the earnings of musicians, the rate depending on the amount earned per week. The tax is highest on radio engagements. The union also derives funds from fines. It pays death benefits to its members, has a hospitalization plan, and operates a relief department.

Despite public criticism of Petrillo, the members of the local support him wholeheartedly and enthusiastically. He has raised the wages, reduced the hours, and improved the working conditions of the union members by significant and substantial amounts. The musicians feel and believe that if there is anyone who can get something for them, that man is Petrillo. There is little likelihood that the membership will turn him out as long as he wants his Chicago job. Formerly, complete reports were made to the local on operations and activities in the *Intermezzo*, the monthly publication of the local; but this newspaper has not been published for several years. The union has flourished during Petrillo's tenure in office. His attempts to enlarge the jurisdiction of the union, however, by including radio announcers and sound effects men proved to be abortive.

Since he was elected to the presidency of the national union, Petrillo has spent much time in New York, where the main headquarters of the AFM are located. He prefers Chicago to New York. Of New York he says: "What a town! Everybody in it's a lawyer. I get to town and sit down, and bam!—there's a dozen lawyers, all tryin' to serve a paper on me."[12] He is the highest paid labor leader in the United States. He receives $26,000 as president of the local plus a contingency fund and, until 1944, a sum sufficient to pay the income tax on this amount. In addition, he has been provided with an automobile, a chauffeur if he desires one, and formerly with bodyguards. On occasion, the local has given him presents of various kinds, such as the money to pay for a trip to Europe with his wife, and a $25,000 summer home in Wisconsin. He can get anything he wants. Since his election to the presidency of the national union, he has received in addition a salary of $20,000 plus a contingency fund and expense allowances which amount to many additional thousands of dollars.

As a family man, Petrillo is a proud father and devoted husband. He was married to Marie Frullate in 1916. One of their sons, Lester, died from football injuries two decades ago. The eldest, James J., is the financial secretary of the Chicago local of the AFM. He has another son, Leroy, and a daughter, Marie. In May 1951, Petrillo set up the Lester Petrillo memorial fund for disabled musicians in memory of his son.

Petrillo generally remembers his own humble beginnings and appreciates the effects of poverty. Sometimes, however, he has become too emotional in an attempt to demonstrate his patriotism and loyalty to the United States. During the second World War he required all orchestras to play the Star Spangled Banner before and after every program. Subsequently, in testifying before a Senate committee in 1943, he magnanimously said: "Senator, the A. F. of M. is second to none in patriotism. If we are needed in the factories, we'll go, including myself."[13]

James Caesar Petrillo looks and acts tough.[14] He is only five feet, six inches in height, but weighs about 190 pounds. During the years in which he has fought for the musicians, he has depended only to a slight extent on aid and support from other labor organizations. The only union which occasionally worked with Petrillo was the International Alliance of Theatrical Stage Employees, whose notorious Chicago leader during the 1930's was George E. Browne. Together they were better able to raise wages in the theaters of Chicago to the highest level in the country.

Petrillo's behavior and actions can be appreciated only in connection with his environment and background. His boyhood and youth, passed in the city of Chicago during an era of violence, racketeering, and labor wars, were marked by personal difficulty and strife. Petrillo found his place amid that turmoil and made his mark. Times of stress call for tough leaders. Petrillo played his part well. As his grip on the industry and on the union became more secure, his attitudes mellowed noticeably. Nevertheless, employers are not yet in a position to take advantage of this apparent mildness. Above all, in evaluating the man, his honesty and his integrity have impressed his opponents. Joseph H. Ream, the executive vice president of the Columbia Broadcasting System, told a committee of Congress in 1948: "So far as I know . . . Mr. Petrillo is always a gentleman."[15]

"... nothing will destroy the usefulness of an organization surer than to set its face against progress no matter how unfavorable we may at present consider same to our interests."

JOSEPH NICHOLAS WEBER

● Motion Pictures with Sound

At first, the strength of the musicians union lay in its control over instrumentalists in the theaters. Before the development of the motion picture industry, the theater orchestras were found mainly in the combination houses where the dramas, musical comedies, and farce comedies were performed. Many additional musicians were employed in the burlesque and vaudeville theaters. Throughout the country there were about 1,000 houses, but the bulk of theatrical employment was provided by about 200 orchestras, each containing, on the average, eight men. (Rarely did a theater orchestra have as many as 15 men.) It was the theater musicians, numbering only a few thousand, who held the most permanent and most desirable jobs in the field of music. Until 1926, they were the most powerful and important element in the musicians unions.

Rendition of music was profoundly changed by the development of two inventions of the late nineteenth century. These inventions, the recording of sound and the motion picture, were both the work of Thomas A. Edison. Though the origin of the record goes back to 1877, its commercial possibilities and uses were not recognized until 1900. The formation of several European companies at that time for the exploitation of this invention was soon followed by similar developments in this country. The American celebrity recordings began in 1903 and during the subsequent decade the emphasis of musical records was on singing rather than on instrumental presentations. But the fidelity of the tone constantly improved and made musical reproductions more worthwhile. In 1913, it was possible to begin orchestral recording. This type of presentation proved to be exceedingly popular.

The effect of these events on the musicians was salutary. The public accepted the record and the phonograph, and they became important household appliances. The result was a wider understanding and appreciation of the various forms of music. The use of records did not curtail the number of jobs available to musicians. Though there were probably many occasions and celebrations when records were substituted for live musicians, the effects of these situations on employment opportunities were more than counterbalanced by the musical education of large numbers of people and the ensuing demand for musical performances. The utilization of records in competition with living musicians did not become a major problem until the 1930's when the radio industry began to place extensive dependence upon the disks.

Recorded music, however, developed in another way in connection with motion pictures. The kinetoscope was invented in 1889 and five years later the first showing of motion pictures took place. Until 1910 motion films were a novelty and were used mainly as an auxiliary feature of vaudeville. But the appearance of the multireel picture in 1909 assured the success of the industry.

One of the first groups to benefit from the introduction of motion pictures was the musicians for the performance of music was necessary to relieve the monotony of pictures which were then unaccompanied by sound. The programs of the picture houses divided themselves into two classes. In one category vaudeville attractions were supplemented by pictures and the regular orchestra was retained. In the other group only pictures were shown but these were accompanied by music. During that early period, stages were not especially built or furnished for the presentation and many stores and halls were turned into motion picture houses.

During the second decade of this century a wave of theater building swept the country. The number of theaters in most towns and cities multiplied. In many instances, the supply of musicians, especially of organists, became inadequate. But the increased demand soon brought on an increased supply, and by the middle of the 1920's an equilibrium had been reached in connection with the employment of musicians in the theaters. The motion picture industry had been responsible for a tenfold increase in the number of musicians employed in the theaters.

Various picture house managers, but particularly Samuel L. Rothafel (better known as Roxy), favored the use of large orchestras, so that in many cases the ensemble approached symphonic proportions. In 1926 there were 22,000 players employed in the pits of theaters throughout the country. They were hired to play appropriate music during the course of the picture.

The existence of the musicians' jobs depended upon the fact that the pictures were silent. Neither music nor words were rendered mechanically. Words were suggested by the addition of titles or brief statements thrown on the screen explaining the action. Music was added by the live musicians. Scientists, however, were engaged constantly to find a method by which the production of both words and music by mechanical means could be achieved.

The theater musicians comprised nearly a fifth of the total membership of the American Federation of Musicians in the 1920's and their solid support gave the union much of the power which it exerted. Suddenly, in 1926, the musicians were struck by the first blow from mechanical music. The potency of the blow was of such force that it nearly shattered the union. Warner Brothers introduced the Vitaphone to New York City audiences. The Vitaphone is a device which synchronizes a disk of phonographic music with the action of the picture by an attachment placed in the booth of the operator. The following year, Fox Film Corporation gave its first public demonstration of Movietone. This invention records the sound on the same film with the motion picture.

Although the installation of sound equipment in the theaters throughout the country was delayed by several factors, eventual utilization of the new devices was inevitable. The leaders of the union hoped desperately that sound projection was a passing fad which would be abandoned by the public after a short trial. Furthermore, Weber did not know what to do and, under those circumstances, he did nothing. The existence of union contracts with the theaters in the United States served to cushion any immediate substantial adverse effects on employment. In many cases, the contract extended for several years and the theater was not able to eliminate the orchestra even if it had that desire. In other cases, however, the theater was able to purchase the contract from the union. The public, in general, did not protest when motion picture orchestras were replaced.

The economics of the situation was the decisive element in bringing about the replacement of musicians. The cost of maintaining an ensemble of only 15 men at an average wage of $60 a week, was $46,800 a year. This figure excludes the salary of the conductor. The cost of installing sound apparatus was from $13,500 to $15,000 for a house seating 2,500 to 3,500; and $9,000 for a house with a capacity of 750 to 1,250 persons. Even when the costs of operations are added the saving to theater owners was obviously enormous. By 1929, 2,000 theaters had been wired for sound pictures.

There were still over 19,000 musicians employed in the theaters in 1929 and they were receiving almost $1,000,000 a week in wages. The next year there were fewer than 14,000 men so employed and the weekly wages had declined to less than $700,000. Since 1930, the number of musicians employed in the theaters has hovered around 5,000. As the volume of unemployed AFM men increased, the power of the musicians union waned. Regretfully, Weber admitted in 1931 that the union had lost its ability to strike successfully. Not a single theater could be closed by the refusal of musicians to work. The substitution of sound pictures for silent films and orchestras had been effectively achieved by the theater owners.

The displaced musicians were unable to find other desirable employment in the field of music. In 1929 there were 20 applicants for every vacancy in symphony orchestras, though three years prior to that time it was difficult for a symphony manager to induce a good theater player to change his job. It is true that the production of sound films opened up approximately 200 new jobs. The studios needed musicians to record the music for the synchronized sound films. But only musicians of the highest caliber could be used for these jobs paying $500 a week. The average unemployed theater musician was not equipped to engage in the delicate work involved.

The scarcity of these recording jobs did not deter many hundreds of musicians from traveling to Los Angeles in the hope of being engaged by the motion picture industry. Almost all were disappointed and disillusioned. After staying for a while, they had to retrace their steps homeward, often being forced to borrow money in order to meet expenses. Weber therefore gave the Los Angeles local special authority to refuse transfer members the right to work in motion pictures.[1] The union desired to curtail the heavy influx of men into that region because it knew that their chances of securing jobs were negligible.

The weakened condition of the union was aggravated by internal dissension, internecine strife, and external pressures. Important elements in the musicians union favored taking the bull by the horns in attacking the problem. Many locals, but particularly the one in St. Louis, wanted musicians to stop recording. They felt that such action would eliminate the production of sound films and restore the theater jobs. The Communists in some of the larger locals proposed that the union should amalgamate with the other entertainment unions in order to gain strength.[2] Weber, however, opposed these factions because he believed that it was impossible to block technological advances permanently. Said Weber: ". . . nothing will destroy the usefulness of an organization surer than to set its face against progress no matter how unfavorable we may at present consider same to our interests. . . ."[3]

It was Weber's belief that since the public would make the final decision a propaganda campaign could succeed in molding and turning public opinion against sound pictures. On the other hand, he feared that any decision to stop recording for films would only lead the motion picture interests to guarantee annual salaries to men who would leave the Federation. It did not appear that it would be too difficult to induce many qualified men to resign from the union in exchange for the high scale offered by the film industry. The Communist arguments, the union heads maintained, were intended merely to disrupt the AFM and were criticized in those terms. The Communists had taken advantage of the difficulties of the union to inflame the members against the leadership, but these radical agitators were unsuccessful. The AFM took a strong position in opposition to the Communist movement during the entire decade of the 1920's.

Weber's grip on the organization, even during this critical time, was complete. His program was carried out in its entirety. The AFM conventions of 1928 and 1929 refused to bar members from playing for mechanical music machines. Instead Weber's propaganda program was adopted. He was authorized to spend considerable sums of money to develop and organize opinion against sound pictures. But as the program was being put into effect the difficulties of the musicians were augmented by the increasing severity of the economic depression. The depression further complicated the employment problem of musicians.

The American press generally has been antagonistic to labor unions. The musicians union however was more highly respected than most other labor organizations. The union was known to carry out faithfully all the provisions in the contracts which it negotiated. The conservative attitude of its leaders had been demonstrated to the satisfaction of businessmen by the experiences of many years. Newspapers rarely criticized the AFM severely. In this respect Weber was fortunate, for success in molding public opinion required the active cooperation of many newspapers. The project he undertook, however, afforded him of itself a partial means of gaining the support of the press.

The publicity campaign against sound movies or "dehumanized entertainment of canned music" began in earnest in 1929. The implications that the struggle was one of workers against machines were avoided. Instead the union expressed its opposition on a cultural and educational plane and offered the opinion that mechanical music tended to debase the art. News stories were released by the union to the press and special articles were prepared for labor newspapers. General criticisms of technological improvements, by other labor leaders were reproduced.

Late in 1929 a systematic advertising campaign was launched. Cartoons ridiculing sound pictures became a regular feature in the distribution of criticism. A publicity firm was engaged and advertising space to present the message of the AFM was bought from 798 newspapers and 24 magazines. The huge expenditures on advertising were responsible partially for the favorable attitude taken by the press towards the union campaign. Large numbers of editorials supporting the union's contention that the public should shun mechanical music appeared in the American press.

That the methods adopted by Weber to combat the inroads of sound pictures on the employment opportunities of musicians were not approved by the entire membership, has been indicated already. Petrillo, it appears, did not agree with the union's arguments against sound pictures. He was not concerned particularly with the fact that music was being debased. Instead, as early as 1929, he expressed the main argument against mechanical music, which subsequently was adopted and is now used by the American Federation of Musicians. He contended that unlike other cases of technological displacement, the musician himself was creating the mechanical device used to replace him and in effect, therefore, the musician was destroying himself.[4] Petrillo argued that the musician had a right to protect himself in these circumstances. Though Petrillo reiterated this argument consistently, it was not generally used by the AFM until he became president.

Early in 1930, the union announced in newspapers throughout the country that it was creating a Music Defense League. In order to join, a person was required merely to sign and send to the union a coupon published in any of the hundreds of papers or dozens of magazines carrying them, in which opposition to the elimination of living music from the theaters was expressed. No obligation of any kind was assumed by the signer. Eventually, over three million coupons of membership in the Music Defense League were received by the AFM.

Perhaps the major accomplishment of the Music Defense League was that it retarded the contraction of employment in the theaters. The success achieved was quite limited, however, as employment in the theaters declined to 4,100 musicians in 1934. The Music Defense League campaign cost the union nearly a million dollars over a two-year period. The propaganda, however, was effective in maintaining public interest in living music. Some support for this conclusion may be derived from an investigation conducted by the inquiring reporter of a New York newspaper in which five of the six people questioned stated that they would prefer to see the return of picture house orchestras.[5] Costs, however, were the decisive factor and the cinema industry was not impressed by mere expressions of preference. Moreover, the position of the union was further weakened by the constant improvements in the production of the music for the sound films.

● *The Union in the Depression*

During this period the national organization encouraged its locals to undertake a project aimed at increasing the public's appreciation of music. It hoped that the project subsequently would create additional jobs for musicians and would relieve some of the unemployment which existed. The project, called Living Music Day, was operated on a local basis. The musicians' local union in any city first secured the cooperation of a local newspaper. This was relatively easy because of the favorable relationship which had been built up during the advertising campaign. The newspaper agreed to print a Living Music Day supplement on a selected day. This supplement contained the advertisements of local merchants, each of whom noted that he was sponsoring a concert in his store on that day. The local unions supplied the bands and orchestras to the merchants without any charge.

The locals were expected to gain increased employment opportunities from the publicity. A Living Music Day was conducted in more than 120 cities and much favorable publicity resulted. Indeed, so widespread was the publicity, that a Living Music Day was held in Johannesburg, South Africa. It is not clear whether there were any important effects on employment even though a few occasional jobs subsequently resulted—particularly in connection with merchandise shows, style openings, and other business and civic events. As a general conclusion, the project was not successful because the original intention of the union to make this event an annual affair was never carried out. Very few locals were willing to repeat the undertaking.

It should not be forgotten that external factors were superimposing difficulties on the problems faced by the union. For the effects of the depression beginning in 1929 continued to become more serious until 1933. Employment opportunities in almost all industries were contracting and unemployment was mounting throughout the country. Many labor unions declined substantially in membership and were considerably weakened; some went out of existence. The musicians suffered also from these general adverse effects. The prevailing economic conditions reinforced the problems arising from technological change.

Some locals in the AFM attempted to alleviate unemployment through various devices. Petrillo's local in Chicago paid out union funds to unemployed members who were assigned to play in the parks and charitable institutions of Cook County, Illinois. In addition, hundreds of baskets of goods were distributed each week to unemployed members of the Chicago local. The New York local also aided its needy members. Throughout the United States, many unemployed musicians were assisted.

The election of Franklin Delano Roosevelt as president ushered in large-scale changes in the American economy and brought about direct governmental attempts to mitigate the general distress which had been caused by the depression. The activities of the federal government primarily affected musicians through the operations of the National Recovery Administration and of the relief programs. Under the NRA, codes of fair competition were drawn up in each industry which, among other things, fixed maximum hours of work and minimum wage rates. The musicians, however, generally opposed operating under the provisions of these codes. Though their union had been greatly depleted in strength during the preceding five years, it was still strong enough to maintain hours, wages, and working conditions which were far superior to those enjoyed by other industries. For example, only rarely did a musician on a steady engagement work more than 40 hours a week; so that a code which set a 40-hour maximum work week was of no benefit to the musicians. The union had little to gain by accepting a code which specified working conditions for industry which were inferior to those it enjoyed already.

The AFM was willing to depend on its own economic strength to achieve its objectives. It feared that if it subscribed to any code containing a minimum wage lower than that which musicians were getting, a tendency to cut wages would be established. Though the musicians union was interested in the radio code, hotel code, and shipping code, it only joined the legitimate theater code. It soon withdrew from that code, however, when the representatives of industry requested an amendment that disagreements between labor and management should be resolved by arbitration. The union did not desire to be guided by the decisions of outsiders. Most of the codes drawn up left the musicians free to negotiate in their accustomed manner.

At the request of the government, the union undertook to stagger employment in the theaters in order to spread the work among a greater number of musicians. Theaters replaced those musicians holding steady engagements every fourth week. An unemployed musician was used as a substitute. The program, however, was designed so as not to increase the cost of music to employers. Shortly thereafter, however, the program was abrogated when it was found that, on a national scale, the staggering policy was unsuccessful. Protests by employers, who objected to the disruption of a well-knit and unified orchestra which resulted from substitution, and discontent among the musicians, who were forced to yield some of their work, led to the abandonment of the plan, in 1934; upon the consent of the Administrator of the NRA. Individual locals were permitted to continue to stagger employment if they were so inclined. Though staggering was common in various industries at that time and was endorsed and approved by a large number of labor unions, it was not applied by the musicians to any other musical field after it failed in the theater.

The relief activities of the federal government were examined carefully by the musicians union. Outright doles to musicians were endorsed heartily by the union. The administration of work relief projects, however, raised some significant issues. The union desired that musicians employed on relief jobs sponsored by the Work Projects Administration should perform work in which they would use their skill, instead of other unrelated work. This proved to be unfeasible on many occasions because some of the responsible administrative officials did not fully support the idea that musical performance should constitute a relief activity.

During the last half of the 1930's the union fought all attempts to reduce the rate of pay of musicians employed by the WPA and objected to Congressional cuts in relief appropriations. It felt that expansion, rather than contraction, of relief work was in order. At the peak of WPA activities, 12,500 members of the AFM were employed by the agency, and an additional 2,500 musicians on the rolls were nonunion members and music teachers.

The union of musicians had passed through a period in which its very existence had been at stake. The decade 1926-1936 was one in which it could not do much more than hold its own. But despite numerous setbacks the AFM was held together by its leaders. Although technological displacement of musicians and the effects of the depression were still serious in 1936, the economic power of the AFM had passed its low point and was on the rise.

The eighteenth amendment to the Constitution of the United States which had been adopted in 1920 had made serious inroads in the employment of musicians, for it had brought an abrupt end in the sale of liquor; and many establishments which had depended on such sale and simultaneously had been employing musicians were forced out of business. But the repeal of the eighteenth amendment by the twenty-first amendment, in 1933, was a herald of returning opportunities of employment in night clubs, cafes, and restaurants serving liquor. The membership of the union, which had reached a peak of 146,326 in 1929 had declined sharply until 1934 when it stood at 101,111. Then it began a slow but steady rise, and subsequently, for a number of years, it showed a tremendous acceleration in growth.

The ability of the union to overcome what appeared to be imminent financial collapse was the single most important factor in giving it renewed vigor and in helping it to re-establish its position. The expenditures of the union had been rising over the years, but the income did not keep pace with the outlay during the depression. In 1932 the main sources of income available to the union were per capita taxes, fines, and conditional membership fees. The per capita taxes collected during those years had declined, however, because of the reduced membership. The chief item of expenditure was salaries and wages of officers and employees. These payments did not decline. As a result the general fund of the union showed a substantial deficit after the operations of 1932. This was also true in 1933.

Under these circumstances, a change of lasting importance was inaugurated in union finances. The laws of the union still required traveling orchestras to charge a fee of 30 per cent over the local scale so that the travelers would be at a disadvantage when competing with local musicians. This money was forwarded to the union and held until the completion of the engagement; it was then returned to the traveling musicians. For many years, however, it was clear to the officers of the Federation that evasion of this law was notorious. Double contracts were used and leaders often loaned the amount representing 30 per cent of the engagement price to the members of the orchestra for temporary payment to the union. National officers therefore urged the repeal of the law. Said the treasurer of the AFM: "I will not go on any further with the detail of this 'nightmare,' but I would ask the Convention to take under serious consideration the question of abolishing the entire 30% law. I am of the firm opinion no one is getting it except those few who would get the same price if the law did not exist."[6] Local unions, however, demurred from agreeing to such action.

Finally a compromise was reached and was put into effect in September 1934. The finances of the organization had been improved somewhat by 1934, because for the preceding two years a two per cent tax had been levied on traveling orchestras; this tax was deducted from the 30 per cent fee sent into the treasurer. But both the 30 per cent levy and the two per cent tax were given up. Instead, a 10 per cent surcharge over local price lists was instituted as the minimum scale for traveling orchestras. This 10 per cent was paid to the local which then forwarded the money to the national treasurer. At the end of the engagement four per cent was sent back to the local, three per cent was returned to the band member, and the remaining three percent was kept by the national union. The enforcement of this rule was much more practicable because the 10 per cent surcharge was not as obnoxious to employers as the 30 per cent levy had been, and attempts to evade payment therefore were not too frequent. The success of this plan soon was established. The general fund was balanced easily beginning in 1935; and the 10 per cent surcharge remained the most important budgetary item of the next decade.

The campaign to increase employment in theaters was intensified in 1936 and 1937. Previously dependence had been placed on appeals to the public. The new pressures were

exerted directly on the motion picture houses. Though undertaken only by the individual locals throughout the country,
these drives received the support of the international union.
The most spectacular events and demonstrations occurred in
New York City. Huge picket lines paraded before the leading
picture houses of the city in an effort to induce the management
to hire live musicians. Near the end of its campaign, the New
York local concentrated its efforts against the RKO chain. The
drive culminated in a theater sit-in strike at the RKO Palace by
200 members of the union.[7] No permanent gains, however, were
registered by the musicians as a result of these efforts.

The losses sustained in theater employment have never been
recovered. At one time musicians had been employed in 4,000
motion picture houses, but in 1950 only 458 theaters employed
them though there were 9,635 houses with a seating capacity of
500 or more persons. Of these 458, 57 used men on a 52-week
basis.[8]

Employment of Musicians in Theaters in 1950

Type of Performance	Number of Musicians	Earnings of Musicians (dollars)
Burlesque	171	526,898
Dramatic and Musical	1,471	2,818,127
Opera and Ballet	808	1,008,405
Organ	18	56,310
Vaudeville and Presentation	1,617	2,656,980
Total	4,085	7,066,720

• Musical Records and the Radio Industry

Gradually the American Federation of Musicians formulated
more complete policies regarding the mechanical reproduction
of music. Primary emphasis was shifted from the theaters to
other employers and dispensers of music. The union desired to
gain greater control over juke boxes, wired music, and radio
stations. It had failed to attain any influence in connection with
the distribution of phonographic records.

The commercial success of the radio industry was not assured
until after it already had been in operation for several years.

The broadcasting industry had its origin in 1920 when the results of the Harding-Cox election were announced on the first nonamateur program, but it was not until 1922 that the first commercially sponsored program took place. The national networks, NBC and CBS, were organized in 1926 and 1927. In the latter year Congress established federal control over the radio. This authority was exercised through the Federal Radio Commission until 1934; and then the Federal Communications Commission assumed jurisdiction over regulation of the industry.

During the early 1920's musicians began appearing on radio programs. They were not paid for their services, but nevertheless felt that the publicity which they received by having their names mentioned on the air was more than adequate compensation for their efforts. Soon, however, the musicians union, on a local basis, established wage scales for radio work and the musicians were expected to adhere to them. Radio stations then found that musical records frequently could be used as a substitute for the personal appearance of performers. It became a common practice to play recordings with the specific intention of misleading the public into the belief that a live rendition was taking place.

The increased use of music records and the misreprensentation as to whether the program was recorded led to the first vigorous protests by the AFM, in 1930, to the Federal Radio Commission. The rules of the governmental agencies supervising radio always have required that when records are played they must be announced as such. The union also attempted to prevent the broadcasters from using phonographic records by having the phrase "for home use only" inserted on the face of each record. The union then encouraged the institution of tests suits in the courts to determine whether a station could disregard the afore-mentioned condition agreed to between the recording companies and the performing artists. During the early cases the union's contentions prevailed. The Supreme Court of Pennsylvania ruled that musicians had the right to prevent the unauthorized use of their recordings.[9] But the federal courts overruled the state courts. The circuit court of appeals decided in 1940 that the property of the orchestra leader in the performance ended with the sale of the records, so that radio broadcasting companies could not be restrained from using the records in broadcasts.[10] It appeared that musicians could not establish property rights in recordings without specific Congressional legislation (such rights have been given to the record manufacturers in England). In the United States, motion picture producers, on the other hand, have had copyright rights to their pictures since 1912. Furthermore, the American Society of Composers, Authors and Publishers has had the right to collect royalties for the use of the songs written by its members. The AFM has opposed the right of ASCAP to make these collections, though it has favored giving a similar power to musicians.[11] Since, however, the union did not have any legal control over the use of musical records by the radio industry, it was forced to take more direct action.

Throughout the 1930's the most vociferous opposition to recordings was expressed by James C. Petrillo. It has been indicated already that he was the first to stress that musicians were destroying their own employment opportunities by making records. But he was also responsible for the first economic pressure exerted against the broadcasters in connection with recordings. In 1931, the Chicago local called a strike of Chicago radio musicians effective at midnight of New Year's Eve. One of the purposes of the strike was to prevent the use of records in commercial broadcasting. But the strike was settled when the stations agreed to reduce the working hours of musicians.

In December 1936, Petrillo took the lead again. He announced that effective the following February 1, in order to end the menace and threat to employment which had been brought about by canned music, the Chicago Federation of Musicians would not permit its members to make any recordings or transcriptions without special permission from the executive board of the local. He recognized that the result might be only to shift recording work from Chicago to other jurisdictions, but he maintained that the musicians could not afford to wait any longer before undertaking an attack on the problem of recorded music. "Someone had to start the move," said Petrillo, "and I believe all other Locals will follow."[12] He was not discouraged by the fact that musicians in Chicago would suffer some immediate loss of employment.

Though Weber may have doubted the widsom of such drastic action by Petrillo, he was forced to approve it. For by the time the June convention rolled around in 1937 some persons felt that Petrillo had become a strong challenger for the presidency of the AFM. At the convention, therefore, Weber commended Petrillo's plan; and then the AFM again endorsed and re-elected its president. Weber received a mandate from the convention to begin a fight on the encroachments of mechanical music.

Weber called in representatives of the radio, transcription, and record companies for conferences. He made sure that they would come by setting a date on which a nationwide radio strike would go into effect if the broadcasters did not attend. He also threatened to halt all recording work by musicians. The union, however, was ready to give up its plan to ban recordings provided it could increase the employment of musicians in the radio stations. Many more than a majority of all radio stations did not employ any musicians, but depended for their music on recordings and on network programs. Neither the radio strike nor the record ban ever was put into effect because the unfolding events led first to postponement and then to abandonment.

The union formulated demands under which every radio station using musical records would place on its payroll a number of musicians acceptable to the AFM. These musicians all were to be union members. Furthermore, no station could transmit any musical program to another station that did not employ musicians. Hundreds of radio stations were represented at the conferences. The representatives of the industry were willing to compromise but for a time they maintained that the stations ought to be permitted to broadcast without any restrictions as to the destination and that it was the union's job, not industry's, to get the small stations to hire more musicians.

After 14 weeks of intense negotiations the AFM reached an agreement with the key stations of the three networks (ABC was not yet in existence) and with the independent network affiliates. The networks and their affiliates had been spending $3,500,000 yearly in wages for musicians. They agreed to spend an additional $2,000,000 on staff musicians, a quarter of this amount being assigned to the key stations of the networks. In 1938, such quota agreements also were reached by the union with unaffiliated stations negotiating through the National Committee of Independent Broadcasters. The unaffiliated stations agreed to expend for staff musicians an amount equal to five and a half per cent of 1937 time sales over $15,000, except that stations whose income did not exceed $20,000 were exempted. The terms of these agreements, which were valid for two years, provided that staff musicians could be used in both sustaining and commercial programs, that stations should not pay rates for musicians higher than those paid by advertisers, and that orchestra leaders' salaries should be counted in the quota.

Subsequently, the Department of Justice advised the parties that the agreements were illegal so that when they expired in 1940 they were not renewed. A precarious armistice existed thereafter; but although the number of radio stations increased, the number of staff musicians declined. Late in 1938 the AFM began licensing companies making recordings and transcriptions. These licenses were contracts by which the companies agreed to employ only union members, in return for which the AFM permitted its members to make records. No musician, however, could work for a company that did not have a license.

● *Other Technological Displacement*

The opinion of the Department of Justice reopened the conflict between the AFM and the radio broadcasting industry. Simultaneously, the union was grappling with other problems raised by mechanical music. The union has had no opportunity to prevent the competition of juke boxes. Though many of the more than a half million juke boxes in operation are located in small establishments and have not displaced live musicians, it may be inferred from the fact that so many machines have been introduced in cafes and restaurants that the jobs of hundreds of musicians have been eliminated. Many of the two- or three-piece bands formerly found in the small towns are no longer used.

The exercise of control over wired music, supplied by the Muzak Corporation, has been somewhat more successful. This service consists of a specially prepared transcription played in a central station and sent over the wires to those desiring this music. Under the contract executed between the company and the New York local of the AFM in 1938, the company stipulated that it would not make its facilities available to any establishment if such action would cause the replacement of live musicians. Since wired music is used in many places which might employ small orchestras, in various instances musicians have been displaced. This is particularly true of the hotel salon ensemble and the restaurant string orchestra. The union, however, has feared to exercise its full rights under the contract because Muzak Corporation might substitute ordinary phonograph records for the special records it now uses. Wage rates paid by the Muzak company were not covered by the local contract, since they are based upon the scales set by the national union.

The union fought a technique by which a great portion of the music used on sustaining programs was not paid for by the radio station. The stations arranged with hotels and restaurants to pick up, by a system of remote control, music played at those establishments. In return, the hotels and restaurants received free advertising when the station announced the place of origin of the music. Musicians, for a short time, received extra pay from the station when it picked up the program. Today, in the jurisdiction of the New York local the hotel pays each musician involved in the remote control broadcast a fee of three dollars above the scale. The money is turned over to a radio remote control fund which is used by the local for the relief of needy members. One of the novel ideas which might have injured the union but which never caught on was a plan to make a film of a band, throw the film on a screen in a hotel restaurant, and play the recorded music of that band. In another area of technological advance, the American Federation of Musicians successfully negotiated with the film industry to prevent "dubbing," the practice of transferring music from one picture to another.

● *The Decline of Weber*

The years between 1926 and 1940 were times of strain for the American Federation of Musicians. At the opening of the period, the union was at peak strength. It completely controlled the rendition of professional music in the United States and dominated most of the American employers of musicians. Then there came a sudden weakening of the union and a substantial decline in membership, which shook the organization to its very foundation. But by 1940 the AFM had recovered most of its former strength and its position was as firm as ever. The musicians union had met and had overcome the twin blows resulting from mechanization and depression. Other unions also passed through a cycle during those years, but in few cases were the effects as vigorous or as significant. Some unions were not able to survive even the effects of one of these forces.

Throughout all this time, Joseph N. Weber remained in undisputed control of the organization. His political acumen and foresight were manifested continually and his annual re-election was a matter of course. Indeed, even during the period when musicians were suffering from heavy unemployment, Weber's salary was increased substantially and his expense allowances were multiplied. There was considerable criticism, but it generally was sporadic, often was incoherent, and never was consolidated. To some extent Weber's control over the AFM was made possible by the rivalry and jealousy between locals. (In 1929 he had been elected a vice president of the American Federation of Labor.)

The musicians union had followed the general practice of labor unions and had remained neutral in politics. But during the period of the New Deal, Weber broke with precedent and supported Franklin D. Roosevelt openly and enthusiastically. It is a curious historical fact that Franklin Roosevelt had been denounced vigorously by this union back in 1914. As Acting Secretary of the Navy he had answered a communication from the Chicago local of the AFM with a routine letter expressing the views of his Department regarding the United States Marine Band. The union then announced that Roosevelt was unfamiliar with the problem and claimed that ". . . Roosevelt . . . was particularly pernicious in his hostility to civilian musicians and could always be depended on to find some technicality or a loop-hole through which the Marine Band and other bands of the U. S. Navy were enabled to continue unfair competition."[13]

But time was moving on, and Weber was getting older. In 1935 he had passed his seventieth birthday. His illnesses and nervous breakdowns had continued to plague him. Almost always the AFM paid Weber's doctor bills and vacation bills. In 1934, the convention of the union ordered Weber and his wife to take a vacation in Europe for eight weeks. It was on the occasion of this voyage that he became better acquainted with

James C. Petrillo. They traveled to Europe together, as the Chicago Federation of Musicians had authorized Petrillo and his wife to take a trip, too. Weber soon was aware of Petrillo's ambition and he knew that Petrillo would succeed him as president.

The clash between these men was soon in the open. Petrillo was younger and tougher. As an exponent of more direct action in solving the mechanical music problem he was more aggressive than Weber. Petrillo's ban of recordings in Chicago had forced Weber to move more quickly to prevent criticism. Petrillo, however, was dissatisfied with the action taken by Weber and the other members of the international executive board in dealing with the representatives of radio and phonograph recorders during the negotiations of 1937 and 1938. He said so outspokenly, and when he was overruled by his colleagues on the international executive board, he boycotted the meetings of the board.

In a front-page editorial in the union publication, Weber attacked Petrillo.[14] Weber denied the correctness of the general impression that Petrillo was the strong man in the union. He was angered particularly at a newspaper statement that: "Petrillo is the 'tail that wags the dog.' What he does for the musicians in Chicago sets the standard for the fiddlers, trumpeters, flutists and accordion players all over the country." Though Weber admitted that the musicians of Chicago were the highest-paid men in the union, he berated Petrillo for being "a self-appointed so-called strong man" and accused him of "dispensing hot air."

As Petrillo's stature increased it became evident that it was only a question of time before he would replace Weber. In 1937 the AFM had set up a trust fund of $250,000 for Weber and his wife. The beneficiaries were entitled to the interest earned by the fund, though this money was deductible from Weber's salary as long as he remained on the union payroll. Finally, at the convention of 1940, the forces behind Petrillo were sufficiently strong to convince Weber to retire. Weber was eased out gracefully from the presidency; he had served for 40 consecutive years, except for one year when he had been in retirement. Weber was made honorary president and general adviser to the union for the remainder of his life and was voted an annual salary of $20,000. He held this position until his death on December 12, 1950, at the age of 85.

Petrillo was elected unanimously as president of the American Federation of Musicians on June 15, 1940. Petrillo was 48 years old at the time.

> *"Senator Clark of Idaho.* . . . But would you not say
> pretty generally that Mr. Petrillo dominates the conven-
> tion of the Federation of Musicians?
> *Mr. Padway.* I would say exactly the opposite; he does not.
> *Senator Clark of Idaho.* I am glad to have your expres-
> sion on that."

• *Centralized Control*

During a hearing before a subcommittee of the Senate Interstate Commerce Committee in 1942, Senator D. Worth Clark
asked Joseph A. Padway, attorney for the American Federation
of Musicians, whether Petrillo controlled the legislative sessions
of the AFM. Padway vehemently denied that such was the fact.
"Senator Clark of Idaho. . . . But would you not say pretty
generally that Mr. Petrillo dominates the convention of the
Federation of Musicians? *Mr. Padway.* I would say exactly the
opposite; he does not. *Senator Clark of Idaho.* I am glad to have
your expression on that."[1]
Both Clark and Padway were aware that Petrillo exercised
considerable discretion and power as head of the musicians
union. Padway, however, was able to express his opinion without equivocation because all of Petrillo's acts as president had
been performed within the framework of the constitution and
regulations of the union and had been approved by the members. Nevertheless, an examination of the constitution and bylaws establishes the fact that power is centralized and vested
mainly in one man—the national president. Petrillo has completely dominated the union. Yet the members of the union
rarely have evinced criticism of their constitution and only
occasionally have they complained regarding the bylaws and
standing resolutions. The members have been behind Petrillo
because he has improved their working conditions and has devoted himself zealously to work for their benefit. Petrillo himself

passionately has denied that he exercises absolute power. He testified before a committee of Congress to that effect in 1948. *"Mr. Hoffman. . . .* You know very well, and everyone in this room knows you are the absolute dictator as to what these locals shall or shall not do. *Mr. Petrillo.* I object to that question. That is not a fair question. *Mr. Hoffman.* That is a matter of opinion. *Mr. Petrillo.* I am not a dictator and I don't dictate to the locals."[2]

The union of musicians always has been strongly centralized and controlled. The first president, Miller, was elected four times and then decided not to run again. Weber held the office for the next 40 years, except during the one year in which he was not a candidate. The authority he exercised over the affairs of the union may be appreciated from a remark he made, when he was ready to retire: "It is with great pride that I am in a position to say that almost all of the recommendations I ever made to the Federation were enacted into laws and almost all of them have achieved the constructive results I expected of them."[3] Petrillo was elected unanimously in 1940 and similar action has been taken each time he has stood for re-election, except in 1949. That year, because of widespread criticism of the lack of democracy in the union's elections, Petrillo was opposed for the presidency at the national convention; but he won overwhelmingly. Indeed, there have been few occasions in the more than 50 years of annual elections, when the delegates to the convention have had a choice among candidates for any of the top offices of the AFM.

The American Federation of Musicians of the United States and Canada consists of locals of musicians and of the musicians themselves. In 1936, the union extended its jurisdiction to copyists, arrangers of music, and orchestral librarians. During the early period of organization both the area of coverage and the membership were expanded until musicians all over the United States, Canada, Alaska, and Hawaii were included. In 1951, the musicians of Puerto Rico affiliated with the AFM. For many years the number of locals has remained approximately constant, although the number of members still is increasing. Until September 1943, some regions in the United States were not in the jurisdiction of any local. But at that time the AFM decided that all neutral territory would be assigned to some local, so that coverage of the country has been completed.

The AFM holds an annual convention in June, and except in 1943 and 1945 when the conventions were canceled because, as a war measure, the government had requested organizations to limit their use of transportation facilities as much as possible, these yearly meetings have taken place since 1896. Each local may send up to three delegates, depending on its membership. The convention is primarily a legislative body and theoretically the supreme organ in the union. It elects the officers of the national union—the president, vice president, secretary, treasurer, and five members of the executive committee, one of whom must be a resident of Canada. All these officers collectively constitute the international executive board.

Though each of the structural units of the AFM has its functions, the powers of the president are so immense that strong central control is established. The relevant provision of the president's authority is in article I, section 1, of the bylaws, which states: "Duties of President. . . . It shall be his duty and prerogative to exercise supervision over the affairs of the Federation; to make decisions in cases where, in his opinion, an emergency exists; and to give effect to such decisions he is authorized and empowered to promulgate and issue executive orders, which shall be conclusive and binding upon all members and/or Locals; any such order may by its terms (a) enforce the Constitution, By-Laws, Standing Resolutions, or other laws, resolutions or rules of the Federation, or (b) may annul or set aside same or any portion thereof, except such which treat with the finances of the organization and substitute therefor other and different provisions of his own making, . . ."[4] Numerous specific duties are detailed, but this general provision gives the president absolute control. These vast powers have been assigned to the president of the AFM since 1919, and although they have never been utilized to the disadvantage of musicians, the president has no clear check on his discretion. In almost all cases where the president has had to make hasty decisions he has consulted and received the unanimous approval of the executive board.

A variety of problems connected with musical entertainment

are of a local nature and a considerable amount of decentralization of authority and power has been necessary in this labor union. However, the union is so constituted that the national organization may wield control over the actions of the local. The national may intervene whenever it feels so inclined, and it has done that in the past. In addition to the enormous powers of the president, the union has several means of guiding locals and members. The *International Musician,* the monthly publication of the organization, has been published since July 1901. It contains much pertinent information regarding union matters. The latest regulations of the AFM are included in a prominent place in the magazine, but material of educational value to musicians also is featured. Minutes of the meetings of the international executive board and proceedings of the conventions are included. There are three regular columns which focus attention on groups ostracized by the musicians union. The journal publishes a list of suspended and expelled members, a national defaulters list comprising the names of employers who have not fulfilled their contracts, and an unfair list containing the names of employers who refuse to deal with the union or have violated some of the rules. Union members may not work for, or with, any persons or organizations named on any of these lists. Each member receives a copy of the *International Musician.* Several years ago, the magazine was revitalized by the appointment of a managing editor.

The president has appointed eight traveling representatives who visit local jurisdictions to establish better contact between the locals and the Federation. They conduct investigations ordered by the president. In addition, an officer is appointed in each state of the United States and in each province of Canada. These representatives protect the interests of the AFM at the state, provincial, and district conferences which are held periodically by groups of territorially adjacent locals to discuss regional problems.

The constitution of the union provides that musicians are members not only of the local which they join, but of the national as well. This provision was inserted to give the national more direct control over the musicians. Formerly conditional members were accepted by the AFM directly when they resided in an area that was unassigned to any local. Since the entire country is now within the jurisdiction of some local, all applicants must join a local union.

Officers of the AFM have the power to prevent any local from violating laws of the national union. Relations with employers which are purely local matters are negotiated and approved by the locals themselves, but all contracts specify that they are valid subject to present and future rules and actions of the AFM. This provision has enabled the national union to pull the locals out on strike even when the local had a contract. Both the president and the international executive board have the power to remove from office a local officer who interferes in any way with the purposes, objectives, or affairs of the American Federation of Musicians.

Although it appears that the annual convention has final authority on all matters concerning the union, this is not strictly correct. The compromise provisions worked out at the time of the formation of the union and written into the constitution specify that locals are permitted one vote for each hundred members, but no more than ten votes, in all elections. On matters affecting changes in the laws of the AFM, each local may, upon roll call, cast as many votes as it has members. But all laws which have been so passed are referred to a convention committee consisting of the executive board of the AFM and the chairmen of all committees appointed at the convention. This group may sanction or veto the law and its action is final.[5] Since chairmen of committees are appointed by the president, the final decision need not have the support of a majority of the delegates. However, this rule which permits the desires of the convention delegates to be circumvented, never has been applied; because roll call votes have not been used.

The power of the union impinges on the employer in ways other than through negotiation. Many employers must be members of the union and others must be licensed by the union. Such requirements are effective in promoting control over the industry. Some employers of musicians, such as bandleaders, play instruments themselves, and they therefore must be members of the union. The first group which was required to obtain licenses from the union, in order to deal with the members, was the bookers. The demand for jazz orchestras in the 1920's led to the establishment of booking offices which furnished em-

Number of Locals and Membership in the American Federation of Musicians in Selected Years[6]

Year	Convention	Number of Locals	Membership
1896	1	26	4,000
1897	2	51	5,979
1898	3	77	9,152
1899	4	91	9,563
1900	5	117	10,176
1904	9	372	37,490
1905	10	402	40,741
1906	11	402	44,451
1907	12	428	47,198
1908	13	481	50,635
1909	14	511	56,961
1910	15	536	56,565
1917	22	703	83,992
1928	33	780	146,421
1929	34	743	146,326
1930	35	736	139,398
1931	36	716	126,423
1932	37	703	118,364
1933	38	684	108,271
1934	39	675	101,111
1935	40	672	102,385
1936	41	641	105,013
1937	42	644	111,960
1938	43	685	124,221
1939	44	712	130,794
1940	45	723	134,372
1941	46	721	137,005
1942	47	718	134,853
1944	48	696	146,772
1946	49	693	181,794
1947	50	704	216,469
1948	51	711	232,370
1949	52	705	237,535
1950	53	698	239,777
1951	54	701	240,269
1952	55	702	242,167

ployers with such bands. Competition between different bookers who sought to gain the commissions paid by musicians for the jobs to which they were referred led to cutting of wage scales. Beginning in 1936, the union has required booking agencies to obtain licenses. These licenses have been confiscated in individual cases for violation of rules. Recording companies were licensed from 1938 until 1943.

• Bargaining Relationships

The union wage policy of the musicians differs from that of most other unions. Usually the output of a plant is directly proportional to the number of workers employed. But musicians normally are hired to work as a unit. The income derived by the employer of a band or orchestra is largely independent of the precise number of musicians in the unit. The union therefore must pay particular attention to the number of musicians employed as well as to the wage rates which they receive. Minimum numbers of musicians are set by locals for different occasions. Where locals have feared that courts would object to contracts which specify a minimum number of men to be employed, they have sometimes worked out sliding scales to induce employers to hire more musicians. At other times, the union has bargained with the employer for a sum of money to be spent for musicians rather than for a specific wage rate. It is significant that though the AFM always has favored the closed shop, it never has tried to dictate to employers the specific musicians to be hired and it never has attempted to protect the jobs of particular instrumentalists. The employer has been free to hire and fire on the basis of merit without any regard for seniority.

The ability to control the members, the locals, and the employers with whom musicians must deal has enabled the AFM to achieve outstanding success in governing employment in the musical field. Improvement of the wages, hours, and working conditions have been steady and at times even spectacular. Though most of the negotiations are done on a local basis, the national sometimes helps the local. The national itself, however, supervises employment conditions for specific groups of musicians. Traveling bands and orchestras are supervised and controlled by the AFM directly. Many of the problems of traveling musicians and bands have been considered in connection with the growth of the organization. This group of instrumentalists includes not only members of name bands, but those in traveling theater companies, grand operas, symphonies, fairs, circuses, and rodeos. Very frequently wages are not negotiated for these musicians, but determined unilaterally by the AFM.

The national union also has concerned itself particularly with radio, recording, and film musicians. The problems raised by radio and recorded musical presentations are of great importance to this union and they are discussed in connection with technological change. The status of musicians in the film industry has never been a serious problem because negotiations satisfactorily have solved most of the matters in dispute.

The musicians union has depended on its own strength in improving the working conditions of its members in the motion picture industry. Although the Hollywood studios are technically subject to the jurisdiction of the Los Angeles local, the AFM has maintained direct control over the motion picture industry from the time it successfully prevented the influx of musicians into Los Angeles during the period when heavy unemployment resulted from the introduction of sound films. As musicians continued to improve their status in the industry, the Los Angeles local, in 1938, prohibited the use of sound track in any picture but the one for which the music was prepared. This made valueless millions of dollars of sound track held by the studios. The producers reduced the size of orchestras partially to combat the effects of the prohibition of dubbing—that is, the rerecording of music from other film.

The first written contract between the film industry and the AFM was signed in 1944. It covered the eight major producers, and prescribed a minimum number of men to be employed in each studio on an annual basis. Dubbing was banned, doubling on two instruments was permitted only if the musician received additional pay, distinctions between work done at rehearsals and in actual performances were eliminated, night work was assigned premium rates, and the remuneration of the leader was increased.

The contract was renewed in 1946, but provisions of substantial advantage to the musicians were incorporated. The three largest producers, Loew's (MGM), Twentieth Century-Fox Film, and Warner Brothers, each agreed to employ 50 men on a yearly basis. Paramount Pictures undertook to use 45 musicians; and Columbia Pictures, RKO Radio Pictures, Republic Productions, and Universal Pictures guaranteed to hire 36 musicians. Wages of film recording musicians, orchestraters, arrangers, leaders, and copyists were increased by 33 per cent and a two-week vacation with pay was granted by the industry. Not only was a clause inserted in the contract which prohibited the use of the musical sound track for any purpose other than to accompany the picture for which it originally was made, but the track could not be used on television. If the producer leased or sold the film, these restrictions had to be assumed by the buyer. The contract was extended for a year in 1948 and was renewed again in 1949 and 1951. At the beginning of 1952 the agreement was renegotiated for a two-year period; the most important change was the provision for a 15 per cent wage increase.

The major studios employ many additional thousands of musicians on a casual basis. These men are film recording musicians, side line musicians, orchestraters, copyists, and librarians; and they make up featured units of name bands, hillbilly bands, and cowboy bands. The terms of the contract are applicable to the entire United States and to Canada. New York City itself provides casual employment for thousands of musicians in the film industry.[7]

In addition to the eight major studios, the motion picture industry contains a large number of independent producers, who in many instances do not have facilities of their own for the production of pictures. When the AFM turned its attention to the smaller companies, they banded together. Four groups of independents were formed. One agreed to employ 40 musicians on an annual basis; these men could be utilized by all members of the group. The other three each agreed to employ orchestras of 20 men. Musicians may work only for companies which have signed agreements with the union. The basic wage rate for a single session of three hours or less is $39.90 per man. In 1948 a new contract for one year was signed under which the independents agreed to employ musicians for at least 35,000 man-hours during the year. This represented a union setback. Beginning in 1952, separate pacts were signed with each independent producer.

The American Federation of Musicians was one of five unions which formed a Motion Picture Internationals' Committee in the movie industry to deal with employers. The carpenters, painters, electrical workers, stage hands, and musicians succeeded in gaining a union shop in Hollywood in 1926 when they signed the Studio Basic Agreement with nine employers. The joint committee which includes also five representatives of the employers, functioned well for a time in adjusting grievances and settling disputes. Later the painters dropped out and were replaced by the teamsters. Subsequently, the committee was torn by strife in a jurisdictional dispute between the carpenters and the stage hands.

- *Relationships with Other Unions—Jurisdictional Disputes and Cooperation*

The musicians union has had little in common with much of the rest of the labor movement. William Green told the musicians that they are different from other unionists who work with their hands.[8] Since the activities of musicians are so unique in the labor movement, the AFM has had few conflicts with other unions on a nationwide basis. The number of alliances and cooperative actions which it has undertaken has been equally small. Dealings with other unions generally have been limited to those unions engaged in some other phase of entertainment.

Only four major disputes with other unions on a national scale have developed in the long history of the AFM; the disagreement with the American Guild of Musical Artists will be considered in another connection. A serious misunderstanding with the Metal Polishers Union (AFL) existed in 1912 and 1913. The metal polishers demanded that musicians should be required to buy and play only those instruments bearing the label of the polishers union. The AFM rejected this demand, claiming that musicians must be permitted to buy the most suitable instruments. The American Federation of Labor supported the AFM in this matter. The dispute ended when the musicians agreed to help the metal polishers unionize the plants of the manufacturers of musical instruments.

A second and more recent dispute has had profound implications. The power and control exercised by the AFM have been so great that the union rarely has had to use the machinery created by Congress to protect the rights of labor. The musicians have not had to call upon the National Labor Relations Board for assistance. One jurisdictional dispute, however, involved not only the NLRB, but the courts as well. A federal court established a principle that would have altered the interpretation of the National Labor Relations Act, had that law not been amended.

The controversy involved the operators of turntables, known as platter turners. These persons place phonograph records on the turntable, adjust the table for speed according to written instructions, and remove the records after they have been played. The operators require neither musical nor technical skill. The National Association of Broadcast Engineers and Technicians, an independent union of radio engineers, has represented the platter turners outside of Chicago at the National Broadcasting Company and the American Broadcasting Company since 1940. In Chicago, Petrillo and the AFM had gained control over the turntable operators in 1927. (The AFM represents the platter turners working for the Columbia Broadcasting System both in Chicago and St. Louis.)

In 1942, the NABET notified the broadcasting companies of its desire to represent the platter turners in Chicago, but was informed that this was not possible since the companies had contractual arrangements with the AFM. The companies, NBC and ABC, subsequently renewed their contracts with the Chicago Federation of Musicians in 1944, and the AFM continued to exercise jurisdiction over the platter turners. The AFM, however, also had made demands. It had asked the broadcasters to hire musicians as platter turners throughout the United States. All the large broadcasting companies agreed and Petrillo estimated that at least 2,000 more jobs for musicians would be created. The union of broadcast engineers was infuriated and countered this move by initiating representation proceedings before the NLRB. It also filed a notice of intention to strike. The Board then conducted hearings and decided that platter turners at NBC and ABC should be included in the unit of musicians in Chicago, but in systemwide units of engineers and technicians, elsewhere. Although the AFM consented to the certification of the NLRB, it threatened the National Broadcasting Company and the American Broadcasting Company with strikes if they recognized the award to NABET. Early in 1945 the National Labor Relations Board, to whom the case returned, found that the companies had violated the Wagner Act by their refusal to bargain with NABET and ordered them to bargain upon request.[9]

The Board petitioned the United States Circuit Court of Appeals for enforcement of its order. The decision of the court upheld the order requiring the companies to bargain, in spite of the fact that the employers maintained that reprisals were threatened by the AFM. Although the broadcasting companies had requested the court to issue a restraining order against the musicians union, the court refused to do so, but said: "If an attempt to prevent the companies from complying with our order should be made it would seem that the ordinary contempt procedures available against a person with knowledge of the decree although not named in it would enable the court to protect its order."[10] It seemed that though the Norris-La Guardia Act of 1932 had barred the federal courts from issuing an injunction or restraining order in cases arising out of a labor dispute, the court was ready to proceed against a union whose objective was to negate a decision of the NLRB, even though a labor dispute was involved. The NLRA had granted neither the Board nor the courts any specific power to act against unions. The matter was never tested beyond this stage, since the AFM bowed to the court's decision. The Labor Management Relations Act of 1947 has made this question academic, because the union now may be restrained.

The most recent controversy involved the American Guild of Variety Artists. It began in 1948 when AGVA, an affiliate of the AFL, undertook to expand its membership. The AFM and AGVA had an understanding that when a member of the musicians union sang, danced, or told stories in a floor show of a night club or on the stage of a theater he was eligible to join AGVA. The Guild tried to get such performers to sign

AGVA contracts for the engagements. On August 5, 1948, the AFM dissolved the agreement with AGVA, warned AFM members that they might sign only AFM contracts, and prohibited musicians from joining AGVA without the permission of the national office.[11]

In December, Gus Van, the president of AGVA, appeared before the international executive board of the AFM in an unsuccessful effort to adjust the dispute. The controversy increased in bitterness at the beginning of the following year when the musicians union charged AGVA with raiding tactics. By September the AFM ordered all members of the AFM who were also members of AGVA to resign from the latter organization, even if they also performed as actors. It served notice on booking agencies that if they insisted that musicians should join AGVA, the license of the agency would be revoked.[12] This ruling forced Tony Lavelli, an accordion player, and Victor Borge, the pianist, to resign from AGVA under the implied threat by Petrillo to strike the orchestras at the places where they were entertaining. Borge explained: "It is easier for me to get along without the AGVA group than it is to do without an orchestra. . . . I can't take any chances."[13] Subsequently, at least 50 artists, including Vaughn Monroe, Artie Shaw, and Spike Jones resigned from AGVA.

The American Guild of Variety Artists applied to the New York State Supreme Court at the beginning of October 1949 for a temporary restraining order prohibiting the AFM to prevent Guild members from carrying out their contract obligations. The treasurer of AGVA said in an affidavit that Petrillo was ". . . obviously overcome with ambition and delusions common to the dictators."[14] William Green, addressing the AFL convention in St. Paul, Minnesota, criticized AGVA for going to court instead of attempting to settle the dispute within the house of labor. The Supreme Court later refused to issue a temporary restraining order, but before the matter of a permanent injunction could come to trial AGVA withdrew its suit in order to resume negotiations with the AFM.

The international executive board of the musicians union left the matter of concluding an agreement with AGVA in the hands of Petrillo in January 1950. In May, an understanding was reached between the AFM and AGVA. Performers who act on some occasions and play an instrument on others would be eligible to join both unions. Instrumentalists who only incidentally act or serve as masters of ceremonies must belong only to the AFM. Actors, on the other hand, who play an instrument during a small portion of the act belong in the jurisdiction of AGVA.[15]

The American Federation of Musicians occasionally has made monetary contributions to support striking unions. In 1910, it helped striking streetcar workers in Philadelphia. The most important link with another union, however, has been a long and pleasant relationship of nearly 30 years with the International Alliance of Theatrical and Stage Employees (AFL). IATSE comprises the stage hands and the motion picture operators. In 1913 these two unions signed a national agreement of cooperation and assistance, although agreements on a local basis already had been negotiated. On many occasions over the years, each of these unions supported the other during periods of critical relations with employers and each conducted numerous sympathetic strikes in the theaters at the request of the other. Together they supported the Actors Equity strike of 1919, which enabled the actors to organize successfully. However, the New York courts denied the right of IATSE to strike in sympathy with the AFM, when an opera company utilized electrically transcribed recordings of the musical score to produce the orchestra accompaniment. In 1941, the Court of Appeals said: "For a union to insist that machinery be discarded in order that manual labor may take its place and thus secure additional opportunity of employment is not a lawful labor objective."[16] The dispute was not settled, however, until 1945. Nevertheless, in spite of the close relationship between the AFM and the IATSE, the agreement between them was abrogated in 1942 when satisfactory terms of a new pact could not be worked out. Over the course of the years, the AFM has not needed much support from other unions.

● *Finances of the National Union*

The strength or weakness of a union frequently may be judged from its financial condition. The AFM has attained the status of financial integrity and independence. Current income is more than adequate to meet the expenditures and the net worth of the union continues to rise. Finance operations are divided among three funds, the general fund, the theater defense fund, and one which now has only slight importance, the recording and transcription fund. The main source of revenue of the AFM is derived from the ten per cent tax levied on traveling orchestras, of which the three per cent kept by the national union amounts to well over three-quarters of a million dollars annually. The other important receipts in the general fund are the per capita tax on the locals, interest on investments, fines levied on members and locals, subscription fees to the *International Musician,* and taxes from radio engagements. The radio tax, a charge of 15 per cent, is paid by traveling orchestras or guest conductors who play a commercial radio engagement over a radio network in another local's jurisdiction. The tax is based on the local's scale price and a fifth of the amount collected is the share which goes to the local. Traveling orchestras, however, may not play any radio engagement which is purely local in character, without the permission of the local which has jurisdiction.

The important expenditures from the general fund are for the annual convention, salaries and expenses of officers, printing costs, rent, legal and auditing expenses, public relations and research expenditures, and per capita taxes to the American Federation of Labor, to the Union Label Trades Department of the AFL, and to the Trades and Labor Congress of Canada. The surplus in the general fund is about two and a half million dollars.

The surplus in the theater defense fund is more than two and a half million dollars. This fund was originally created, in the early 1920's, to provide a source of money which could be used to pay strike benefits to theater musicians. Two per cent of the salary of all theater musicians was paid as a tax to the union; and in 1929 this levy was also imposed on those musicians making sound pictures. Locals receive five per cent of the amount collected. Over the years, however, the size of the fund continued to swell because the volume of strike benefits paid was small. In 1946 the convention removed the tax from musicians employed in the theaters and the international executive board reduced the rate paid by those making sound pictures to one per cent. This fund is utilized so sparingly that it continues to grow rapidly.

The recording and transcription fund has fluctuated widely in amount. It comprised the moneys paid to the union by the recording and transcription companies and was based on the sale of records. The fund reached a peak of several million dollars, but has nearly been exhausted as the AFM allocated the money to the locals so that they could present free public concerts and provide employment for musicians. Under contracts with the recording and transcription companies, negotiated at the end of 1948, a new fund outside of the control of the union has been established.

The AFM has achieved and maintained an excellent record in presenting the membership with all the pertinent data regarding the union's financial transactions. Expenditures made by the AFM were considerably more itemized until the end of 1936, but nevertheless the reports are still fully satisfactory for most purposes. The financial strength of the union has been an important factor in the exercise of control over the members. The union has never had any national insurance schemes, though it unsuccessfuly attempted to establish an old musicians' home in 1903. The AFM has made provision for the payment of strike benefits on all occasions when it calls musicians out on strike and especially for payment of benefits to striking traveling musicians. The ability to make such payments has earned the respect of the members and the employers. The mere availability of the money frequently has removed the necessity of striking to gain objectives.

The AFM has fixed the maximum initiation fee which locals may impose at $50. Though it does not tell the locals what dues to charge, it has levied a per capita tax of a dollar and sixty cents per member per year upon the locals, but this amount also covers subscriptions to the *International Musician*. This sum is one of the lowest union per capita fees levied by any international. Since many musicians are not professionals and derive only occasional income from music, the AFM and its locals have had to depend largely on other sources of income.

Since the passage of the Social Security Act in 1935, the identity of the employer of musicians for purposes of paying the various taxes under this Act has not been clear. The union has contended that the person who hires the leader is the employer. Some of the persons affected by this rule have not always acquiesced. However, for many years all leaders but name band leaders were exempt from the taxes. By a decision of the United States Supreme Court in 1947, however, all leaders were deemed to be employers for purposes of social security taxes as long as they organize an orchestra and hold it available for limited engagements.[17] Organized orchestras as well as name bands are included, regardless of the prominence or income of the leader. As a result, the leader, rather than the purchaser of the music, has become responsible for the taxes.

The subsequent interpretations of the Commissioner of Internal Revenue of the United States Treasury Department have varied. But near the end of 1947, he decided that, on the basis of the court's ruling, the only leaders whom he would not consider employers are leaders of staff orchestras in radio stations and theaters and leaders of orchestras organized by an establishment or person to play permanently at that establishment or for that person.[18] This interpretation has been challenged unsuccessfully by the union.

In order to compensate the leaders for the increased financial burden which the decision of the United States Supreme Court imposed upon them, the AFM authorized the locals to alter the form of the standard contract so that either the purchaser of the music would agree specifically to accept liability for retirement taxes, unemployment taxes, and income withholding taxes; or, as an alternative, the locals were permitted to increase the wage scales so that a sum of money adequate to cover the tax liabilities of the leader would become available to him.[19]

● *Sundry Problems*

On a national scale, the AFM has been enmeshed in various problems only some of which were related to music. Apart from its stand on immigration which has been considered in connection with the importation of musicians, the AFM followed the line adopted by many other unions in the 1920's and expressed its strong denunciation of Communists and communism. Communists, Fascists, and Nazis are ineligible to join the union, and members may be expelled for holding such views. Unfortunately, however, the AFM had to depend upon the support of Father Charles E. Coughlin in order to make an editorial comment regarding the concentration of wealth in the United States.[20] On the other hand, Petrillo indicated in 1949 that he would not permit Wilhelm Furtwaengler, German conductor charged with having figured in Nazi concerts during the second World War, to conduct the Chicago Orchestral Association.[21]

Petrillo has argued that individuals have the right to free speech. The cross-country trip of Senator Robert A. Taft at the end of 1947 enabled many organized workers to express the bitter resentment which had been aroused by his sponsorship of the Labor Management Relations Act of 1947. Every time he stopped along the route to deliver a scheduled address, Senator Taft was met in force by labor pickets. The president of the Des Moines local inquired of Petrillo whether a band of 26 pieces hired to play in connection with one of these speeches should take part. Petrillo replied, in effect, that musicians should pass through the picket lines if necessary to fulfill the band engagement. He declared that Americans have the right of free speech, even if their ideas and opinions are disagreeable.[22]

The affiliation of Negro musicians has been a more delicate problem. Though in most Southern regions, Negro members must be affiliated through subordinate locals, this practice was followed also in many Northern cities. Some locals in the North, accepted Negroes on a basis of equality. In others, they were forced into subsidiary locals whose policies and activities were determined by white locals. It was only at a time when the federal government was fighting the practice of discrimination against the employment opportunities of Negroes that the international executive board, in 1944, canceled the charters of 12 colored locals operating under control of white locals in their jurisdictions and chartered them directly. In 1940, the New York local forced the Decca Company to withdraw from sale a record which the local claimed was degrading to Negroes, entitled "WPA." During 1942 and 1943, Negro and white musicians working for the Ringling Brothers circus went on strike for higher wages. The national union refused to settle the strike when the owners agreed to raise the wages of the white musicians. The union demanded that the wages of both groups should be increased. Eventually the salaries of the white musicians were raised from $47.50 to $54.00 per week while those of the Negroes were increased from $26.50 to $30.50. In 1946, the AFM convention canceled its outing in St. Petersburg, Florida, after it was advised by local officials that the color line must be observed in that city on all visits made by the delegates. Today the AFM has more than 50 colored locals, of which the largest, the one in Chicago, has over a thousand members.

Public attention has been directed in recent years to facts which have established that some musicians have utilized drugs and narcotics to improve their performances. In 1947 the convention of the AFM gave the international executive board power to expel all members convicted of being drug addicts.

The musicians union has not maintained a consistent policy regarding the teaching of music in schools and the musical training and education of children. Although it has not permitted children to be used in professional bands and in competition with adult musicians, it has been undecided as to whether music should be taught in the public schools. The union has been somewhat fearful that the stimulation of musical interest among public school students unduly increases the number of potential musicians. Even today the policy of the organization on this matter is uncertain.

The tactics and policies of the American Federation of Musicians has enabled it to succeed in gaining control of musicians in the United States and Canada. But it has never been very important in Canada. Although it began chartering Canadian locals in 1900, it was not until the Toronto convention in 1913 that a resolution was adopted changing the emblem of the AFM. All reference to nationality was removed, for the old emblem had contained the figure of the flag of the United States. In 1946, the union had only 6,713 members in Canada, and in 1947, it had 8,108 members. In 1951, there were 30 locals and more than 10,250 members in that country.

The American Federation of Musicians has to some extent been organized along the lines of the medieval guilds and has exercised control over purchasers of music, leaders, conductors, bookers, and musicians. At all points, the person who wants to have any dealings with professional musicians comes in contact with the AFM. The national union permits the locals to exercise much discretion but it intervenes whenever it feels that such action is necessary.

"During the past ten years we have not granted a single concession."

WILLIAM FEINBERG

• *The Consolidation of the New York Local*

The greater proportion of contacts between the employer and the union occur on a local basis; fewer meetings are held between employers and the national officers. The power wielded by the organized musicians may be understood only if the activities and functions of the locals are examined. The AFM includes locals of all sizes. The 31 largest locals, each having a thousand or more members, cover all the important jurisdictions in the country. There are hundreds of medium-sized locals, which though lacking the prestige and authority of the larger ones, constitute the heart of the Federation. Small locals, those with a hundred or fewer members, are dominated by the national, a condition which permits the national to exercise control over the affairs of the union. The more than 200 small locals, however, do not contribute significantly to the progress of the union.

These different-sized units are not comparable in the scope of their activities. The larger the local, the more complicated is its structure and organization, and the more numerous are its functions and operations. The larger locals are located in the more populous cities, where a greater number of musicians is needed because the types of performances are more diverse and the occasions on which music is used are more frequent. Although a description of a large local necessarily would not be typical of the AFM, it would indicate, however, the range and complexity of the tasks performed. Obviously a local with 50 or 60 members could not be very active in labor relations and its dealings with employers generally would be highly informal.

Membership in the 20 Largest Locals of the American Federation of Musicians, 1951[1]

City	State or Province	Local	Membership
New York	New York	802	30,964
Los Angeles	California	47	13,456
Chicago	Illinois	10	11,850
Detroit	Michigan	5	5,013
Philadelphia	Pennsylvania	77	4,889
San Francisco	California	6	4,543
Cleveland	Ohio	4	2,503
Milwaukee	Wisconsin	8	2,476
Pittsburgh	Pennsylvania	60	2,377
Boston	Massachusetts	9	2,367
Toronto	Ontario	149	2,270
Miami	Florida	655	2,179
Newark	New Jersey	16	1,897
Montreal	Quebec	406	1,887
Seattle	Washington	76	1,864
Minneapolis	Minnesota	73	1,744
Washington	District of Columbia	161	1,539
St. Louis	Missouri	2	1,477
St. Paul	Minnesota	30	1,345
Kansas City	Missouri	34	1,288

The New York local, the Associated Musicians of Greater New York, Local 802, AFM, is by far the largest union in the Federation. It is a well-rounded organization and demonstrates how an efficient unit should operate. The early history of the organization of musicians in New York City already has been described in connection with the National League of Musicians of the nineteenth century and the struggle between the locals and the national during the first part of the twentieth century.

When local 802 was organized in New York in 1921 the national union made certain that it would retain control of the new unit. The constitution of the local was framed to provide that a majority of its governing board would be appointed by the national union. The declared objective of this arrangement was to eliminate the possibility that a situation would recur in which the group in power could violate the laws of the AFM. But there were many persons in the local who were anxious to gain autonomy. As the New York unit grew and as the years passed, the demands upon Weber and the international executive board by these members became more vociferous and their cries for autonomy became louder. Weber was adamant, however, and refused to relinquish control.

Some of the musicians who demanded home rule, and who had been opposed to Weber from the days of the struggle of 1920 and 1921, complained to Congress. A Congressional committee was investigating industrial and labor racketeering in the early 1930's and upon the request of musicians it held a hearing on the relationship between the national union and local 802.[2] The unfavorable publicity resulting from the investigation forced Weber to modify his position and he decided to permit the local to elect its own officers at the end of 1934. They assumed office in 1935. The president, however, remained an appointee of the AFM for another two years, and retained the power to veto all local actions which in his judgment violated the laws of the national. Much of the success of the local dates from that time when the membership repudiated the officers appointed by Weber and elected those men who had fought for autonomy. Edward M. Canavan, the appointee who had ruled the local as chairman of the governing board became one of Weber's assistants and until he retired in 1950 was one of Petrillo's assistants. The traces of animosity between the national union and local 802 still are evident though complete formal cooperation between them exists. At the 1951 convention of musicians, Charles R. Iucci, secretary of the local, was elected to the international executive board. This marks the first time that local 802 has had a member on this board.

The elected officers of the local include the president, the vice president, the secretary, the treasurer, nine executive board members, nine trial board members, and a number of delegates to conventions and labor bodies. All have terms of two years. The nine executive board members together with the four major officers constitute the full executive board, the highest body in in the local. General supervision over the affairs and property of the local is vested in the executive board. It has the power to approve or disapprove all contracts and all leaders who hire members of the local for professional engagements and it may demand payment from the employer in advance.

The trial board of nine members has original jurisdiction over all cases involving infractions of the local laws and regulations, and over all violations of wage scales and working conditions. Charges against members or employers may be brought by any union member. Appeal from the decision of this board may be taken to a membership meeting or to the international executive board. The members of both local boards receive $125 a week. They must devote full time to the affairs of the local and may not accept any professional engagement during their tenure of office.

The biennial election of officers arouses the keen interest of the membership and involves a vigorous campaign and election. Candidates and their supporters engage in much political activity and electioneering. Balloting is supervised entirely by the Honest Ballot Association; the local itself has no jurisdiction. From 1935 until 1953, one group was able to retain control of the organization, and in general gained each victory by a substantial margin. This party has represented the more conservative element in the local, but nevertheless has introduced many progressive ideas. A second party represents a more leftist point of view and comprises a greater proportion of the younger musicians, including many of the veterans of the second World War. To some extent this group, not holding office, has been able with convenience to propose greater benefits for the membership and stronger resistance to employers. A third faction comprises the Communists, their sympathizers, and the more radical veterans, but has been relatively weak. Although charges were made by the losers that there were irregularities in the method by which the Honest Ballot Association conducted the elections of 1942 and 1944, these claims could not be substantiated. Court action to upset the election of 1944 was withdrawn by the plaintiffs. The conflict within the local usually gives way on matters in which the national union is concerned, however, and even the extremists usually support the international president, James C. Petrillo.

By the middle of 1948 it was clear that renewed internecine strife on a major scale had broken out in local 802, preliminary to the biennial elections. The group in power accused its opponents of being led and dominated by Communists. It enacted a rule that all candidates for office must sign affidavits that they are not Communists. The membership meetings of the local became exceedingly bitter. The operator of the hall rented by the local to conduct these meetings protested to the union that fighting between members had occurred, that police and detectives had to be summoned on several occasions because of disorders, and that his property had been damaged. The executive board of the local set aside several decisions made by the members, but on an appeal to Petrillo by the insurgents some of the rulings of the local board were overturned.

Richard McCann was re-elected president of the local in December 1948 but by a mere majority of 89 votes out of a total of more than 10,500 ballots cast. The opposition group claimed that the election results had been tampered with, despite the fact that balloting had been under the control of the Honest Ballot Association, and asked the international executive board to set aside the vote. The AFM, however, turned down the appeal.

The friction in local 802 continued. In the autumn of 1949, two members of the local who had distributed leaflets maintaining that McCann was a defender of "Ernest Bevin's policy of antisemitism" were expelled from the local by the trial board after being brought up on charges. At the beginning of 1950, however, a membership meeting of the local at which about 900 persons were present overruled the trial board and reinstated the two musicians. McCann then appealed the reversal to the international executive board. Though the board sustained the appeal, it nevertheless refused to expel the two members of local 802. Just before the local elections in 1950, McCann decided to retire. His party, however, continued in power until 1953, when some high offices were won by opposition leaders. At the convention in 1951, Petrillo took note of the conflict within the local and indicated that something would have to be done about the Communist agitation there.

Most of the members are satisfied that local 802 is operated democratically. The important activities and decisions of the local are reported in the monthly publication, the *Official Journal,* now entitled *Allegro.* Detailed minutes of the meetings of the executive board are included in the bulletin. The secretary must make a semiannual report to the members and the treasurer must submit a detailed quarterly certified statement setting forth the financial condition of the local. The membership generally is lethargic. Though the union schedules a meeting each month under a constitutional provision, and advertises it widely, a quorum rarely is present. Five hundred members out of the more than 30,000 in the local constitute a quorum, but in 1946 only three meetings were held. Indeed, this number was so unusually high only because it was a year marked by strikes. In 1947, poor attendance by members made it possible for only one membership meeting to be held. Today it is still very difficult to assemble a quorum. The power to approve proposed changes in the price lists and bylaws, which is vested in the members who take part in the monthly meetings, is conferred upon the executive board when a quorum does not appear. The officers of the local generally have been able to carry out their own programs.

● *Collective Bargaining*

Musicians are hired by many kinds of employers. They are used in symphonies, in theaters, in operas, for recordings, for wired music, in hotels, for dances, for funerals, in the open air and indoors, and on land and sea. Engagements are considered steady if musicians are employed on five days a week for at least one week or on three days a week for two or more weeks. All other types of tenure are single engagements. Because of this diversity of employment conditions, the rules and laws of the local must be complex.

New York City practically is a closed shop for professional musicians. Since musicians are educated and developed without any relation to union policies or to training programs by employers, the union must admit them on relatively easy terms or else face competition from nonunion musicians. The examining committee which passes on the qualifications of applicants acts in a purely perfunctory manner. The New York local, like the others in the AFM, is open to membership. Although the important employers of musicians have been unionized for many years in New York, a campaign to organize the smaller and the occasional employers was undertaken by the new administration in 1935. To aid in this task, a branch office was opened in Long Island, New York, as an adjunct to the main Manhattan office, because the local has jurisdiction over Nassau and Suffolk counties as well as over the five boroughs in the city. The campaign was highly successful in achieving unionization.

The local does not negotiate with all who desire to hire musicians. Instead it sets the price in advance and an employer must pay the scale fixed by the local or go without musicians. In dealing with the important and organized employers, the union does bargain collectively. Among such employers are the theater operators, hotel owners, motion picture houses, symphonies, and opera houses.

Local 802 has fought hard in negotiations with the employers. William Feinberg, formerly secretary of local 802, in summarizing the activities of the local, wrote in 1945: "During the past ten years we have not granted a single concession. On the contrary, every time a contract has come up for renewal, we have fought for and obtained improved conditions."[3]

Collective bargaining with the theater owners is typical of the labor relations of local 802, although employment of musicians for this type of work is particularly peculiar to New York City. New York City has 30 legitimate theaters all of which are represented by the League of New York Theaters. Among the represented theaters, 15 are operated by the Shubert interests, four by City Playhouses, and 11 are independent.

The local and the League negotiate a wage scale and some working conditions, though most of the conditions of employment already have been determind by the union in its rules. The value of the trade agreement from the point of view of the employer is that it gives some stability to the industry and prevents the union from making constant changes.

Plays are classified as dramatic, musical, or drama with music. It is in connection with the latter category that controversy arose. Some people were shocked when local 802 decided to consider such plays as Maurice Evans' *Hamlet, Androcles and the Lion,* Shakespeare's *Henry VIII,* Shakespeare's *Tempest,* and *Happy Birthday* to be musicals. The producers asked the union to designate a third category for plays with more music than the usual overture, entr'acte, and exit march of the drama, but less than the usual score of standard musicals. Music in these plays is not incidental, but an integral part of the production. The union obliged and designated a category known as drama with music, in which the musicians remain in the pit throughout the show, but the employer avoids the necessity of hiring the number of men required in a musical. On several occasions the international executive board has set aside decisions of the local with regard to the classification of specific plays.[4]

The rules of the union designate the number of men to be hired for each type of play. Musical plays given in theaters seating under a thousand persons must utilize a number of musicians determined specifically by the executive board. If the theater holds between a thousand and 1100 people, 16 musicians must be employed. Larger theaters must use at least 22 men. Dramas with music take six musicians and pay the wage scale of the musical. Dramas having incidental music employ four men, but at a lower scale. If no music is included in the play, musicians need not be hired in New York City; although in other jurisdictions a minimum number of men must be employed regardless of whether there is music in the play. In January 1951, the National Labor Relations Board ruled that the demand by a local of musicians that a theater employ a greater number of men than the operator desired did not violate section 8 (b) (6) of the Taft-Hartley law—the featherbedding provision—as long as the union actually was seeking to increase employment. In May 1952, a lower court reversed the Board.[5] On March 9, 1953, however, the United States Supreme Court upheld the Board's decision.

The union has imposed additional regulations upon the theater operators. At least four union men must be employed when mechanical musical devices such as records and radio music are utilized in the play. The union requires that the contract for the season should be signed by the theater before Labor Day. Otherwise a penalty wage scale applies and wages are increased considerably. But those theaters paying a penalty scale during one year must continue to do so if the same play is performed, even if the contract for the following year is signed before the September deadline of that year. The number of musicians in a musical may not be reduced by the producer during the first six weeks of the run even if originally set above the union's minimum, but subsequently may be cut to the minimum if notice is given two weeks in advance. The leader or contractor receives one and a half times the scale of the ordinary musician and the conductor one and three-quarters times the scale. In practice, the remuneration of the conductor almost always is much more than the minimum.

One related incident which aroused national attention occurred at the Mansfield Theater in January 1942, during the performance of the play, *In Time to Come*. The producer utilized recordings to play the Star Spangled Banner and other musical selections in the play. Local 802 demanded that four musicians should be hired by the producer, since under its rules dramas with incidental music must employ at least that number. When the employer refused to hire musicians because he maintained that they were unnecessary, the local threw a picket line around the theater. Mrs. Eleanor Roosevelt, who had tickets for one of the performances, refused to cross the picket line. In her daily column she expressed surprise at the union's demand.[6] This incident focused national attention on the practices of requiring standby bands and of enforcing featherbedding demands used by the musicians union.

Some of the requirements and regulations of the local are obvious illustrations of featherbedding, but the union has been powerful enough to impose such conditions on the employers. The League of New York Theaters bargains to determine wage scales paid by theater operators. The scale for traveling theater musicians, over which the local does not have jurisdiction, is fixed by the AFM. The national union fixes the scale, it does not negotiate.

The local is faced with the problem of preventing kickbacks. Sometimes employers have an understanding with musicians that part of the salary is to be returned. On other occasions, each musician hired gives part of the wages which he receives to the leader. Many such cases have occurred and continue to occur in the theaters and other types of musical employment even though it is a violation of the laws of the State of New York.[7] Progress has been made by the local in eliminating this practice, but intensification of the kickback occurs as economic conditions deteriorate and unemployment among musicians increases. Kickbacks are not unusual today. The union requires that copies of all contracts entered into by musicians must be filed at its office, and the union itself now is a party to all agents' contracts. There is a standard union form of agreement which must be utilized and which helps the local police the industry. The requirement that contracts must be filed is particularly important to the union because of the prevalence of small employment units where irregularities and violations of union regulations are most likely to occur.

Only with great difficulty did the union organize the dance field. Years of militant pressure, boycotting, picketing, and policing were necessary. Hotels, cafes, night clubs, and taverns are grouped in Class A, Class B, or Class C depending on their ability to pay. Each class has its own wage scale. Single engagements, which occur mainly in catering halls and hotel ballrooms, came under the union scale slowly, and only after many leaders were expelled and many agents and bookers had their licenses revoked. Today all major ballrooms are required to employ a minimum number of musicians on all occasions when music is utilized.

The scale on the general single engagement in the larger establishments is $15 per man for a three-hour period during the day or $20 on weekdays and $24 on Saturdays for four hours of evening performance. Rehearsals must be paid for separately, and overtime is computed at the rate of five dollars per hour on weekdays and six dollars per hour on Saturdays. Scales on steady engagements vary widely depending on the type of performance, but those musicians holding permanent positions are among the highest paid group of workers.

Though the caterers who owned or had concessions in the different establishments at first were reluctant to come to terms with the union they began to adjust themselves to the new conditions once they made agreements. Each caterer had a group of preferred leaders whom he had recommended to customers engaging his establishment to run an affair. The local considered this practice to be monopolistic and attempted to eliminate the influence of the caterer in determining which musicians should be employed. It prohibited caterers from giving leads to those interested in hiring musicians. The caterers protested to Petrillo, however, and the international executive board overruled the local.[8] As a result, the caterer may recommend a band or an orchestra to the customers, but he is prohibited from forcing them to accept his designations.

A serious conflict developed between the musicians and the hotel operators in 1946. Musicians' wages in hotels had been rising rapidly and the hotel owners, through the New York State Hotel Association, refused to grant the full increase demanded by the union that year. Local 802 struck in over 50 hotels in New York City. Petrillo immediately brought the national union to the support of the local. He pulled out the musicians from hotels in Chicago and several other cities which were linked by common ownership to the hotels involved in the New York strike.[9] The Muzak Corporation cut off wired service to those hotels and the International Brotherhood of Electrical Workers (AFL) assured local 802 that it would not install any juke boxes. After two and a half weeks the union gained most of the demands it had presented. But the strike cost the local over $80,000, of which more than $26,000 were spent for strike benefits and over $37,000 were paid out to pickets. Additional smaller gains have been made since that time. In 1951, the National Labor Relations Board reaffirmed its policy that hotels are not subject to the Taft-Hartley law.[10] This ruling permits the union to impose featherbedding provisions providing the state law does not ban the practice.

Local 802 bargains with the independent radio stations in New York City. In the spring of 1950, the most important stations in this category agreed to contribute three per cent of the scale paid to musicians into a fund to finance health and hospitalization insurance for musicians. Radio station WINS, however, refused to agree and dropped the eight musicians which it had employed from its payroll. The union struck against the station and placed WINS on its unfair list.

WINS asked the court for a restraining order against the picketing. This request was granted in April. In May, the court approved a temporary injunction against the union because it did not find that a labor dispute existed. Subsequently, however, at the end of September the New York State Supreme Court refused to grant a permanent injunction and ruled that the union may picket the station.[11] It held that the musicians were involved in a dispute with the station. It was not until April 1951 that the strike was settled. WINS agreed to rehire

YOUNG JIM PETRILLO IN 1919

PETRILLO WITH PRESIDENT TRUMAN AND GLADYS
SWARTHOUT AT A FREE CONCERT SPONSORED BY THE
AFM IN WASHINGTON, D.C.

PETRILLO GREETS PRESIDENT EISENHOWER
AT AN AFL CONVENTION

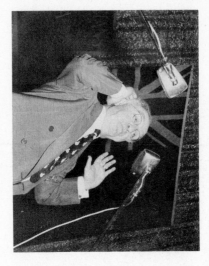

PETRILLO IN ACTION AT AN AFM CONVENTION

eight musicians at the previous wage scale and to pay into the fund the same percentage which the other stations were contributing.[12]

● *The Attack on Unemployment*

In an industry where much of the employment is of a casual nature and where many thousands of persons are not professionals, there usually is a considerable amount of unemployment. Local 802 has used various tactics to increase the employment opportunities of its members. The union has encouraged summer band concerts in the public parks. With the cooperation of the city, with grants from a foundation, and with the support of various merchants and business concerns, these concerts have been given annually since 1938, in increasing numbers. Considerable employment and income have been provided for many musicians.

Since 1947, the moneys allocated to the local from the recording and transcription fund and more recently from the music performance trust fund—the funds based on the payments made by the record and transcription companies—have provided many jobs for union members. The musicians have spent these funds in sponsoring thousands of free public concerts. Many different types of performances have been held.

Local 802 has attempted to eliminate the practice by which musicians play without remuneration. Rigorous control is exercised over rehearsals and the musician generally must be paid when performing in them. The union recently has established the general policy that no free music may be supplied by any musician to any organization on any occasion unless the other goods and services utilized at the function, such as food, hotel space, printed materials, and waiter service, are also obtained without any cost by the organization making the request for the music.

On several different occasions the local has made attempts to spread the available work among a larger number of musicians. For a time, doubling on instruments was prohibited. Today the practice is permitted, but penalty rates are imposed on the employer. The local tried to prevent those with steady jobs and in the higher salary range from taking additional work, but the protests were so loud and sustained that this plan was abandoned. Furthermore, eleven members of the union were given permission by the international executive board to take the case to court. As a result the local enacted a resolution that any members having steady engagements of five or six days in any week may not play on any of their off days. Though the executive board attempts to enforce this rule very strictly, infractions have been common. No penalties have been imposed because members are lax in bringing charges against the violators.

Membership in Musicians Unions in New York City for Selected Years[13]

Year	Local	Membership
1903	310	3,500
1913	310	5,100
1921	310	8,000
1921	802	12,000
1928	802	15,500
1930	802	17,000
1934	802	15,273
1937	802	17,766
1940	802	21,335
1943	802	22,092
1945	802	24,686
1947	802	28,771
1950	802	30,560
1952	802	30,746

Local 802 has been successful in reducing the seven-day work week of musicians to one of five and six days without permitting employers to cut wages correspondingly. In the last few years it has also been able to induce several groups of employers to grant vacations with pay. This victory marked a milestone in the history of the musicians union. Many of the concessions won by the local have tended to increase the employment opportunities of musicians.

Like the other locals, 802 has grown rapidly in the last 15 years and the problems of unemployment thereby have been intensified. As a result, an old and troublesome grievance has been revived. As the number of transfer members coming to the New York local has mounted, local 802 has expressed its opposition to the policy of the national which permits the unrestricted movement of members of one local into the jurisdiction of another local. However, there is little that it can do to bring about any changes in the bylaws of the AFM.

While the union definitely discriminates against nonmembers, there is no discrimination because of race, color, or religion. For many years, Negroes have constituted about ten per cent of the membership. The local has no special problems connected with racial or religious antagonisms, even though cliques based along such lines exist. On the other hand, every effort is made to eliminate the competition of expelled and nonunion members. At the end of 1948 the local prohibited student bands from performing at college games played at Madison Square Garden. It held that the matches were business ventures for profit, and that professional musicians should be employed.[14]

The union has appointed stewards and business agents to police those employers whose labor practices are questionable and to organize the unorganized. The *Official Journal* of the union which contains much information of value to the members and is one of the better union publications in the United States, publishes a supplementary unfair list of local 802 and a list of expelled members. It has printed photographs of musicians who played in an establishment at a time when it was being picketed, under the caption—dishonor roll. These musicians have been barred from membership by the local.

In pursuing its objectives, local 802 occasionally receives help from other unions. It has been indicated already that the electrical workers agreed to cooperate during the hotel strike of 1946. The musicians local had an informal alliance with the waiters, cooks, and bartenders during the period when intensified pressure was applied to unionize hotels and night clubs. On a more general basis, regular delegates are elected to the New York State Federation of Labor, to the Central Trades and Labor Council, and to the United Hebrew Trades. Dues are paid to the Negro Labor Committee and to the Jewish Labor Committee.

Difficulties were encountered in relations with the International Brotherhood of Teamsters (AFL) in 1941. The New

York local of teamsters announced that when out-of-town bands arrived at theaters in taxis and buses, their instruments would have to be carried across the sidewalk by union teamsters at a charge of ten dollars in the daytime or twenty dollars at night. The musicians refused to agree to this procedure, and the teamsters threw picket lines around the theaters. Petrillo ordered his men to disregard the pickets. "Can you imagine them guys?" he said. "They was being unreasonable!"[15] The policy of the local has been to permit members to use their own judgment whether to cross picket lines set up by other unions. Musicians are not ordered to do so by officers of the local.

The musicians union has no control over the training of instrumentalists. At any time, many thousands of persons who are capable of earning their livelihood as musicians do not choose to do so. If opportunities in the field of music become more favorable—and they generally have been since the end of the war—new members join the local to take advantage of economic conditions. The test given by the examining committee is generally no obstacle to admission and the new men soon are seeking jobs and therefore tending to increase unemployment. It is difficult to estimate how many members of the local are unemployed because a large number of them are not professional musicians and may have jobs in different types of production and enterprise. The membership of the local has expanded rapidly and has kept pace with the growth of the national.

● Finances

The financial operations of the New York local, which are of considerable magnitude, have helped to establish a favorable record for the local. When autonomy was achieved in 1935, the bank balance of the local was just over $3,000 while the total amount of unpaid bills was nine times as large. Reorganization of the finances helped achieve a sound and stable position. Like the national, 802 publishes comprehensive financial figures. Quarterly and annual statements, audited by certified public accountants, are printed in the *Official Journal*. At present the surplus of the local, which has been declining for several years, is about $425,000. At the beginning of 1952, the local increased the annual dues by $8, though on previous occasions the members had refused to authorize a change. The local has for some time been seeking means to enlarge its revenues, so that the annual deficits may be eliminated.

The receipts of the local are derived from various sources. All applicants for membership must pay an initiation fee of $50. The dues of $24 a year which members pay constitute the single main source of revenue. Though these payments are considerably lower than those levied in other national unions, especially when account is taken of membership privileges derived by musicians, the local has imposed a one per cent tax on the scale price of all engagements. This tax is levied also on the salaries paid to officers and employees of the local who are members of the AFM. This method of raising money is equitable because many musicians are not employed constantly at the trade. Hence they have no tax to pay during the time they are not working as musicians. In addition, the levy is imposed only on the scale established in the price list so that those earning above the scale need not pay on the amount in excess. This tax does not affect the top artists of other locals who play in the New York jurisdiction, and although the solo artists of local 802 are expected to pay the tax, no issue is raised if they do not.

Thousands of dollars are collected annually as fines for the late payment of dues, fines imposed by the trial board, initiation fees, and reinstatement fees. Investments yield some interest and dividends, and advertising in the journal accounts for a few thousand dollars. Local 802 receives its share of three taxes imposed by the AFM—traveling band tax, radio tax, and theater tax. Union receipts during the year exceed a million dollars.

The union provides a variety of benefits to the members. All regular members are protected with a thousand dollar life insurance policy even if they contribute nothing more than the annual dues. The insurance is paid by the Union Labor Life Insurance Company. Indigent and unemployed members are provided with relief. Originally relief was financed by a relief and organization fund which derived its income from a three per cent tax imposed on all engagements. But in 1943 this tax was abolished by the membership. However, at the insistence of the union leaders the one per cent tax already described was substituted; though this income is not used for relief.

Members over 50 years of age, who have been in the union at least ten years and are in need, are eligible to receive relief. They receive up to seven and a half dollars a week. The money in the relief fund is derived from the radio remote control charges. The local reserves the right to require recipients of relief to perform work around the office, and assigns them to do clerical work or to serve as doormen, investigators, or pickets. Senile members receive donations. At the peak, 2,000 musicians were on relief, but even during the prosperous year of 1947, 800 of them were being assisted. The figure has remained relatively stable since then.

Members on the relief rolls, and some who are in financial need, are entitled to the benefits of the medical and hospitalization plan. The local pays the Manhattan General Hospital $20,000 a year, so that relief members may obtain without any charge, district doctor service, hospitalization, specialist care, X rays, medicines, and vaccinations, whenever necessary. Formerly, members not on relief were eligible to take part in the medical plan if they paid a special fee, but they were barred subsequently because the scheme did not work well and because the hospital was not favorably disposed to their participation.

Union lawyers are available to members whenever they have difficulty in collecting wages and salaries. The local has a special department which performs the task of collecting claims and remitting the money to the appropriate members. A veterans bureau was established in the union to assist members discharged from the armed forces who have personal problems. Unlike the AFM, local 802 has no standard provisions regarding strike benefits. Although strike benefits usually are paid when the members are called out, the executive board of the local determines the amount as each specific occasion arises.

The Associated Musicians of Greater New York, Local 802, presents a picture of a thriving and active organization; but it recently has been pervaded by fear and despair that the increased use of recorded music is making the musician obsolete. Though its activities and operations are quite extensive, basically it attempts to raise and protect the wage scales of the membership. The New York local typifies operations in their most complex form. Few other locals in the AFM engage in activities on so vast a scale. But in its own way, and within the framework of the rules and regulations of the AFM, each local must solve similar labor problems. A description of the methods used by, and the behavior of the New York local helps to gain an understanding of how other locals manage their affairs.

"He's [Petrillo] a very able man in his line. For his
union he did a splendid job."

SERGE KOUSSEVITZKY

● The Change in National Leadership

Weber had the qualities needed by a good leader and he was
able to build the union from a small organization into a huge
and successful enterprise. But by nature he was cautious and
slow to act. It was his policy generally to gather, sift, and weigh
the facts in each situation carefully before making any major
decision. As a result, many tasks which should have been undertaken and problems which should have been considered, but
which were not critical at the moment, were pushed aside. Only
in an emergency did he show boldness and daring.

Persons who knew Petrillo expected more aggressive action
from the musicians union after the change in leadership in
1940, and they were not disappointed. Petrillo has been more
willing to take a chance and more likely to act impetuously. He
has been more familiar with what he wants than Weber had
been. It was not long before employers, union members, and
the public realized this.

Petrillo had taken up the struggle against the mechanical
reproduction of music and musical recordings in his own local
in the 1930's, but his success in this matter had been quite
limited, for he had tried to deal with a national problem on a
local level. Nervertheless, his exceptionally successful leadership
of the Chicago local and his outspoken statements somewhat
had annoyed Weber and a few other leaders in the AFM, and
they had rebuked Petrillo severely. But he had remained un-
daunted.

Although the other national and local officers of the American Federation of Musicians understood that the unrestricted
use of records might reduce the employment opportunities of

THEATER   MUSIC

Operatic Un

Rebirth of Orchestra Under Reiner Stirring Up New Excitement

By Claudia Cassidy

PERHAPS THERE IS a tide in the affairs of music, which, taken at the flood, leads on to opera. Perhaps that tide is rising now. I am not sure of it, and I have my fingers crossed. The last time it surged up here was when Artur Rodzinski, restoring the Chicago Symphony orchestra to its rightful place, set the town in a tizzy with that unforgetable "Tristan and Isolde" celebrating the return of Kirsten Flagstad. Now, when Fritz Reiner is making that orchestra a magnet for audiences who had all but given up hope, the operatic undercurrent is getting too loud to be ignored.

Not that it involves Mr. Reiner except by implication and wishful thinking, unless we can make him twins. He has his hands full. Take a good look some of these days at the orchestra's schedule, and multiply it by a man of meticulous craftsmanship who has an artist's fierce pride in shining acomplishment. Sooner or later, he will give us opera from the stage of Orchestra hall. Later, perhaps, in the opera house. But right now, whether he knows it or not, he has done more to stir up operatic excitement than any man since Rodzinski.

On the Aisle

The reason is simplicity itself. People have discovered, or rediscovered, that the way to have something in Chicago is to do it ourselves. Visitors are fine, we love them—well, sometimes we love them. But to count on visiting orchestras to delight us while we are bored to death with our own—that nonsense of painfully recent vintage is past and gone. We have always had one of the richest orchestras in the world, now again we have one of the finest. Week after week it gets more exciting to hear. The idea could be—I think it is—catching.

Loop Movie Schedule

CHICAGO — "**Half A Hero**," a comedy drama about a young couple, Red Skelton and Jean Hagen, trying to make ends meet.

EITEL'S PALACE—"**Cinerama**" a new form of film projection on a wide, concave screen, which provides an illusion of both depth and roundness, without the use of glasses. The program is in color and has high fidelity, directional sound. Tickets are sold on a reserved seat basis.

GRAND—"**All the Brothers Were Valiant**," a tale of love and intrigue on the high seas, in color. Robert Taylor, Stewart Granger, and Ann Blyth are the stars.

LOOP—"**Martin Luther**," a portrayal of the beginnings of the Protestant Reformation. Niall MacGinnis plays the title role.

McVICKERS—"**Botany Bay**," a sea adventure story, in color, based on the novel by Charles Nordhoff and James Norman Hall. Leading players are Alan Ladd, James Mason, and Patricia Medina. Co-feature: "**Flight to Tangier**." Joan Fontaine, Jack Palance, and Corinne Calvet co-star in this story of murder and espionage in North Africa. In color.

MONROE — "**Torch Song**," in color, is the love story of a musical comedy star, Joan Crawford, and her blind pianist, Michael Wilding.

ORIENTAL—"**How to Marry a Millionaire**." Marilyn Monroe, Betty Grable, and Lauren Bacall star in this comedy about girls, men, and millions. In color and CinemaScope, a wide screen process which does not require the use of glasses.

ROOSEVELT—"**The Big Heat**," a story of crime and gang rule, co-starring Glenn Ford, Gloria Grahame, and Jocelyn Brando. Co-feature: "**The Forty-Ninth Man**," starring John Ireland and Richard Denning, tells how, under cover of "war games," an A-bomb is smuggled into the United States. Coming Wednesday: "**99 River Street**," with John Payne and Evelyn Keyes.

STATE-LAKE — "**The Robe**," dramatization of novel by Lloyd C. Douglas, starring Richard Bur-

JACK
CARSON
"the marriage fix"

8:00
WBBM-TV
CHANNEL
2

SUNDAY

THE
GENERAL GE **ELECTRIC**
THEATER

musicians, they had not been able to decide what should be done. Weber and his assistants were not sure how to proceed. They agreed that the musicians could not undertake a fight to block the production and utilization of recordings. As a close student of labor history, Weber was familiar with the decline and demise of unions, like those in the glass industry, which had fought technological advancement. But though the AFM sought a solution to this problem for nearly 15 years, it did not succeed in finding one. No means of control were discovered, that were both practical and legal.

The new president was ready to throttle the recording industry. It was clear to him that musicians were losing work and that job opportunities were being curtailed as a result of the use of records. Now, for the first time, he had the whole organization of musicians behind him, and he prepared to fight the recording companies. It was Petrillo's belief that, as a general principle, the production of musical recordings must be terminated. There were, however, in 1940, two important weak spots in the plan he had formulated to ban recordings which he had to overcome before the program could be undertaken.

● *The Dispute with the American Guild of Musical Artists*

Two major groups of musicians were not controlled by the musicians union at that time. First, solo instrumentalists and their accompanists were not members of the AFM and, secondly, the members of the Boston Symphony Orchestra had never been unionized successfully. These two gaps in the exercise of control over American musicians by the union had to be closed if success in the elimination of recordings were to be attained. Otherwise, the companies would be able to produce a large number of musical disks by utilizing these nonunion sources of music. Within days after his election to the presidency, Petrillo turned his attention to the removal of these obstacles to his plan.

In 1896, the AFM had been given, in its charter from the American Federation of Labor, exclusive jurisdiction to organize performers on musical instruments. But the musicians had not seen fit to organize the instrumental virtuosos of their profession. The musicians believed that this group could be organized only with great difficulty and that no advantage was to be gained by having them in the union, since these artists were neither competing with ordinary musicians nor lowering standards. Subsequently, when the American Guild of Musical Artists was organized as a labor union in 1936, it tried to enroll concert and opera singers mainly, but accepted and encouraged solo instrumentalists, accompanists, and symphony orchestra conductors to join. Only a number of the solo instrumentalists, however, became members of AGMA. At no time did the AFM clearly relinquish its jurisdiction over the solo instrumentalists, though there is little evidence that any strong protests were made by the musicians union during the period when AGMA began to organize them.

Early in August 1940, Petrillo decided to act. Since the long-range program of the musicians union required that the union should exercise some control over the instrumental soloists, Petrillo ordered this group of musicians to join the AFM by Labor Day. He warned that unless it did so, members of the musicians union would not be permitted to play at any function in which soloists participated. In his letter to Lawrence Tibbett, president of AGMA, Petrillo stated that the instrumentalists and symphony leaders must resign from AGMA and join the AFM. He maintained that the policy of the AFM required these individuals to join the labor union which had jurisdictional rights. The musicians union formulated this position in an attempt to prevent a gradual infringement on the area which had been assigned to it by charter and to restrain the excesses of AGMA. Notice of the union's position was sent to radio networks, opera companies, symphony orchestras, and others who might be affected.

Overnight the incident raised a national issue. The contesting personalities were colorful and the names of the leading musical artists of America were involved. The nation chuckled when Petrillo said: "Since when is there any difference between Heifetz playing a fiddle and the fiddler in a tavern? They're both musicians."[1] Describing the action of AGMA, he said: "They went along and took the instrumentalists. They took the piano players and then they took orchestras. They stole my people and I'm going to get them. They're musicians and belong to me." Tibbett and Petrillo discussed the matter for two weeks and it appeared as if some progress was being made towards an amicable settlement. The leader of the musicians seemed willing to compromise.

But Lawrence Tibbett secretly was preparing a court case. AGMA had worked diligently and laboriously in building its membership to 1,800 persons and was not willing to relinquish any part of it. Tibbett was no doubt aware that the proper tribunal for adjudicating and adjusting the dispute was the American Federation of Labor. But past experience had demonstrated that the more powerful labor union usually wins its case before the councils of the AFL. His own AGMA had absorbed a smaller AFL union through use of some highly questionable legal technicalities on a previous occasion.[2]

The American Guild of Musical Artists asked the court to restrain Petrillo and the musicians union from carrying out their threats against the instrumentalists. Justice Ferdinand Pecora of the New York Supreme Court granted a restraining order, which barred Petrillo from taking any action in the matter until a regular session of the court could hear the case. Great astonishment was expressed by the judge that the president of the union had the authority to impose fines on members of the union and to suspend or change any provision of the union constitution, at his discretion.[3] These provisions were not new, of course, for Weber had been vested with similar powers for more than 20 years. It was not unexpected therefore that the American Federation of Musicians turned down Pecora's subsequent offer to mediate the dispute.

In a statement to the press Tibbett declared that the battle between AGMA and AFM was not jurisdictional, but the beginning of a fight for freedom of musical culture in America from petty totalitarian dictators. Meanwhile, the position of AGMA received general approval. Tibbett was unanimously elected president of the American Federation of Radio Artists. The Screen Actors Guild came out in support of AGMA. The newspapers of the country generally were behind the Guild. Pleaded Petrillo: "Everybody calls me the tsar, the chieftain and this and that. What can I do?"[4]

As both sides prepared for the next step in the court test, the musical artists laid plans to stage a mammoth fund raising concert which would include performances by Jascha Heifetz, Efrem Zimbalist, Mischa Elman, Jose Iturbi, Lily Pons, Gladys

Swarthout, Ezio Pinza, and Kirsten Flagstad. This concert was never held, because many of the stars involved were uncertain which side to support on the issue.

In the middle of November, Judge Aron Steuer of the New York Supreme Court rendered a decision which set aside the temporary stay of action granted previously, but at the same time he stated that AGMA could have the issues in the case tried in court. He declared that though members of the AFM might be under dictatorial control and exposed to the danger of union extortion, these facts were outside the scope of judicial notice.[5] AGMA announced its intention to appeal, and Petrillo assured the court that the matter would be held in *status quo* until the case would be reviewed by a higher court.

The Appellate Division of the Supreme Court affirmed the decision of the lower court in refusing to grant the Guild an injunction, but went beyond that and held that since a labor dispute was involved no cause for action could be found; and it dismissed the case against the musicians.[6] This decision was unanimous and clear-cut. When the AFM decided that solo instrumentalists must become members of the union by March 1941 if they desired to perform with other musicians, the rush to enroll began. Though only a few soloists met the announced deadline, more than a hundred of the leading instrumental artists in the country and many symphony conductors joined the musicians union in the next few months. Some of them had previously been members of AGMA and some had never been in any union before. Sergei Rachmaninoff, Fritz Kreisler, and Josef Hofmann were given honorary memberships by the musicians. They were excused from initiation fees and dues, but agreed to conform to the laws and rules of the union. Four instrumentalists who were not United States citizens and therefore not eligible to join the union, and a minor, likewise ineligible, were given permits by the Federation of Musicians when they agreed to adhere to the rules of the union.

Albert Spalding, who was one of the founders of the Guild, resigned from that body and joined the Federation. He told the press that while the original purpose of the Guild had been to form an organization of solo singers and instrumentalists, AGMA had proceeded to organize chorus members, dancers, and accompanists, so that instrumental soloists had become only a small fraction of the total membership. In addition, he said, the soloists had been asked to employ only Guild members as accompanists. Spalding then declared that the court rulings were decisive and that he was joining the musicians union; his attorneys had assured him that there was no basis for the fear expressed by some persons that onerous terms and conditions would be imposed by the AFM on the instrumental soloists.

Petrillo had won a resounding victory. The important solo instrumentalists in the country were members of his union. The Department of Justice then announced that a federal grand jury would investigate charges that Petrillo had conspired with radio chains and concert booking agencies to destroy AGMA. The Department was interested in the arrangement under which most of the concerts presented in the United States were controlled by NBC and CBS. The networks were able to do so through a technique by which Civic Concerts and Community Concerts, affiliates of NBC Artists Service and Columbia Concerts Corporation respectively, supplied only block-booked schedules. The investigation was to cover the practices used by booking agencies, concert bureaus, and broadcasters in dealing with artists in the musical fields and it was to examine the relationship between Petrillo and these organizations. The investigation, however, was never made.

When the New York Court of Appeals, highest court in the state, ruled in the summer of 1941 that the Appellate Division had erred in dismissing the case against the AFM, AGMA already had lost the instrumentalists. The Court of Appeals held that though it was proper to vacate the temporary court stay, a trial should be held as to whether the musicians should be prevented from taking over the soloists and whether they should be required to pay damages. The court stated that the broad doctrine had been established with regard to labor unions in the State of New York that harm intentionally done is actionable if not justified.[7] Justifiable harm—some activity having a reasonable connection with wages, hours, health, safety, the right of collective bargaining, or other condition of employment—would be a lawful labor objective. No such objective was obvious to the court in this case and therefore a trial should be held. The decision, however, had come after the AFM had consolidated its hold on the solo instrumentalists, and though

AGMA did prepare for trial the outlook for the eventual success of the Guild was hopeless.

During the winter of 1941 the American Federation of Musicians finally moved in the direction which it had previously rejected. It asked the American Federation of Labor to revoke the charter of the Associated Actors and Artists of America (Four A's), the parent organization of AGMA, for trespassing upon the jurisdiction of the AFM.

The AFL is vested with the power to take such action. A union joining the labor federation receives a charter in which its organizational jurisdiction is outlined. Exclusive rights to organize certain kinds of workers are granted and no other labor union in the federation may infringe on these areas. The AFL has the authority to enforce and revoke the charter if a union violates any of the provisions. Unfortunately the record of the American Federation of Labor on matters jurisdictional has been dismal. Economic power usually has been the only determinant upon which it has based decisions in jurisdictional questions and disputes. This weakness displayed by the AFL has been the cause of much public criticism and concern and has led to legislative intervention.

When Petrillo asked the American Federation of Labor to investigate his charges that AGMA had transgressed jurisdictionally, William Green, president of the AFL, advised him that the unions should try to settle their differences through amicable negotiation. The musicians union had won the struggle and was interested in obtaining general acceptance of its new position. The Guild desired to salvage what remained of its former control. A settlement was reached in February 1942 after weeks of negotiation. It provided that AGMA would recognize the AFM's jurisdiction over concert solo instrumentalists and accompanists in all fields. AGMA, however, received authority to act as the exclusive bargaining agent for all the solo instrumentalists when they were engaged in the concert field only and it was permitted to control the relationship between these musicians and their managers.[8] The New York Supreme Court lawsuit which was pending was discontinued. Even as agreement was reached, Petrillo was able to state that 99 per cent of the solo concert instrumentalists were already members of the American Federation of Musicians.

Both the AFM and the AGMA had been subjected to strong criticism during the controversy. Petrillo, however, had borne the brunt of the abuse. He had been threatened and reviled by an indignant press and an aroused public. Nevertheless, as the courts ruled in his favor and, subsequently, as a settlement was reached with AGMA, there was a considerable tempering of the attitude of the public and even an expression of occasional words of approbation for Petrillo. AGMA, though subject to much less censure, had not escaped unscathed. During the preceding years its activities, as well as those of its parent body—Associated Actors and Artists of America, had been marked by conflict and turmoil. The battle with the stage hands in 1939 had been one which aroused resentment and bitter enmity. These facts were not forgotten by those persons who denounced the actions of the Guild.

The outcome of the solo instrumentalist case strengthened Petrillo's hand immeasurably. He was in much more strategic position with regard to his objectives in the field of recordings, and furthermore he could hasten the completion of his negotiations with the Boston Symphony Orchestra which he had undertaken and which was part of the larger plan.

● *Unionization of the Boston Symphony Orchestra*

The Boston Symphony Orchestra was founded in 1881. It was organized by Henry Lee Higginson, whose name is often prefixed by the title "major" because that is the rank he attained in the army during the American Civil War. Higginson, a member of a banking family, had considerable wealth when he launched the orchestra. He had been a music enthusiast during his youth and in his later years he desired to build an orchestra which would be worthy of the highest merit. In the nearly 40 years of his association with the orchestra, he preferred to be its sole underwriter. During that span of time he met deficits aggregating nearly a million dollars from his personal resources.

The beginning of Higginson's long struggle with the union came shortly before 1890 when a new conductor of the orchestra was to arrive from Europe. The local musicians union objected to the admission of this conductor to the United States on the ground that his entry would violate the alien contract labor law, but the contention was not sustained. Though this incident preceded the organization of the American Federation of Musicians it is illustrative of what was to follow.

By the turn of the century all of the symphony orchestras in the United States except the one in Boston had been unionized. Higginson hated and resisted labor unions, and in order to stem the tide of union affiliation which he foresaw coming towards his orchestra, he introduced a pension plan in 1903. Nevertheless a large number of the members of the Boston Symphony joined the union by 1904. Higginson warned the members of the orchestra that if the union interfered in any way with his policies, he would disband the symphony. The men who had joined all resigned from the union.

The union, thereupon, turned its attention to the task of eliminating a major source of the supply of musical talent for the Boston Symphony Orchestra. This source was the foreign musician. Though the musical critics agreed that many foreign instrumentalists displayed a higher caliber than those residing in the United States, the union denied this assertion. The union, on the other hand, maintained that foreign musicians tended to undercut American wage standards. It therefore did not permit any person to become a member unless he had declared his intention of becoming an American citizen and had obtained his first papers. At the union's Boston convention in 1906, President Weber said: "It is about time to give the American boy a chance in America."[9] The union claimed that foreign musicians were recruited only because the practice made it possible to include elements of novelty in the season's preliminary press notices; but that no improvement in the orchestra resulted from the annual changes in personnel.

It is possible that the superior achievements of the Boston Symphony might have been attained by depending solely upon American musicians. But leadership among symphonies could not be maintained if the orchestra were confined in its recruitment to nonunion musicians. Except for members of the Boston orchestra, the best musicians in the United States generally belonged to the American Federation of Musicians. Since members of the AFM could not be easily persuaded to join him, it was incumbent upon Higginson to seek replacements and new performers for his nonunion orchestra abroad. This process effectively thwarted the union in its efforts to gain control over the Boston Symphony Orchestra, even though it had a closed shop in the other symphonies performing in the United States.

During the years preceding 1920, the Boston Symphony reached the height of its musical eminence under the leadership of Dr. Karl Muck. Muck had been the conductor of the Royal Opera in Berlin for 20 years when he was given permission by the German Emperor to go to Boston in order to lead the orchestra in that city. He remained in Boston during the seasons of 1906 and 1907. Muck then returned to Germany to fulfill his contract there, but he was again attracted by the much greater financial remuneration offered in the United States; and he resumed his leadership of the Boston Symphony Orchestra in 1912.

Early in the first World War, Muck was criticized severely for presenting "all German" recitals. After the United States entered the war, it became customary for all orchestras and bands to play the Star Spangled Banner during each program. Muck refused to comply with the public request that the Boston Symphony adopt this custom and as a result set in motion a wave of nationwide criticism. Higginson and Muck argued that the national anthem was not suitable for symphony presentations. Higginson threatened to disband the orchestra rather than to allow it to play the anthem. Muck, however, became the center of the storm when Walter Damrosch declared that Boston's conductor was a loyal citizen of Prussia.

The mayor of Boston, James M. Curley, ordered the license of Symphony Hall canceled if the orchestra failed to play the anthem at every performance. The American Federation of Musicians congratulated the mayor on his patriotic stand. Under the severe public criticism the orchestra abandoned its first position and agreed to play the Star Spangled Banner, but the action came too late to save Muck. A few persons came to his defense, but almost everybody else resented his attitude. The Swiss legation in this country verified the fact that Muck was a citizen of Switzerland. But since he had been born in Bavaria, had been associated with Germany for the greater portion of his professional life, and was conducting an orchestra which, because of the foreign background of its members could not be considered American, he became a symbol of the enemy. He was arrested as an enemy alien and jailed. When the war ended he was released from internment and went back to Germany. He refused many lucrative offers to return to this country. In 1939, the year before his death, he was decorated by Adolph Hitler.

Although Higginson was strongly pro-Ally, he endured personal humiliation during the war because of the loyalty he manifested to his conductor. When Muck was interned, Higginson, then 83 years of age, announced that others would have to carry on the burden of supervising the affairs of the orchestra and he severed his connections with the symphony.

After Muck was arrested, the managers of the symphony, in order to appease public opinion, discharged all members of the orchestra who were citizens of enemy countries. These men were unable to secure new employment because they were not members of the union. Union membership was a prerequisite for all of the better jobs available to musicians in the country. The National Alien Enemy Relief Committee requested the union to admit these men to membership. Weber denied the request because it required action that was in conflict with the principles under which the union operated. No musician imported under a contract could become a member of the union because contract labor represented unfair competition. The union maintained that members of the Boston orchestra had been recruited in this unfair manner and that if they were permitted to join, others would be encouraged similarly to violate union rules. The National Alien Enemy Relief Committee accepted this explanation.

The most nearly successful attempt to organize the orchestra prior to 1940, occurred in 1920. An attempt to unionize the group had been made by some of the members in advance of the opening of the 1918-1919 season. Management met this challenge by giving all the instrumentalists in the orchestra a bonus of $250 for the season. This action ended unionization efforts. Similar methods had been used by the orchestra to frustrate union plans five years before.

Early in 1920, 80 members of the Boston Symphony Orchestra requested the nine trustees to increase wages and at the same time took steps to join the union. It was already clear that the new management of the orchestra was also opposed to the union. Judge Frederick P. Cabot, chairman of the board of trustees, had threatened to disband the symphony if any signs of unionism were manifested. When he had been told by a committee of musicians the preceding year: "We can't live any more these days on the salary you pay us," he replied: "Well, gentlemen, all I can say is that you had better change your profession."[10]

The members of the orchestra had valid grievances. The minimum wage paid to the members of the Boston Symphony Orchestra was $35 a week. But in the other symphony orchestras, all of which were unionized, the minimum was $55. Cabot estimated that the wage demand made by the players in 1920 would increase expenditures by $100,000 and declared that the trustees were in no position to make this additional outlay. Though he declared that the orchestra's wages were 30 per cent higher than before the war, he did not mention that the cost of living had doubled. Cabot, however, told the men that union membership would not be an issue providing they were willing to accept the open shop principle. Under no circumstances would he recognize the union, since that would give it some control over the orchestra.

It has never been established definitely whether the will of Higginson had determined in any way the attitude that the trustees took towards the union. Higginson had died in the interim between his retirement and 1920. Though he had at one time announced that his will provided $1,000,000 to perpetuate the symphony, he revised the instrument during the Muck affair. Then he added several codicils. The probate of the will showed that nothing was left to the Boston Symphony, but in one of the supplementary documents he left his valuable musical library and musical instruments to the orchestra contingent upon the discretion of the executor who between three and five years after the testator's death was to make or cancel the gift, "guided by the manner in which the Symphony Orchestra shall have been and is being managed."[11] The trustees might have been influenced by this provision.

The management remained adamant in its refusal to deal with the players even though 90 per cent of the orchestra, including Frederic Fradkin the concertmaster, had joined the AFM. Suddenly Fradkin was discharged, ostensibly for disobeying the conductor. Over 30 men struck to secure his reinstatement, but Fradkin succeeded in getting them to return to their jobs. The trustees, however, withheld the pay of these men pending disciplinary action. The men promptly struck again and with the help of local musicians organized their own orchestra and actually presented several concerts. The Boston police, however, prevented the strikers from picketing the Boston Symphony Orchestra.

The revolt of the union members fizzled out. The trustees remained firm. The press was united in opposing the strikers. The public was apathetic regarding the entire question, just having witnessed the abortive Boston police strike of 1919. And the Boston Symphony left for a road tour after successfully replacing the strikers. Former members of the orchestra were rehired. New recruits were sought and found. Then some of the strikers resigned from the union and rejoined the orchestra. By the end of the summer the complement of men in the symphony was once more complete.

The Boston Symphony was not to regain its prominence as one of the world's leading orchestras until Serge Koussevitzky assumed the leadership in 1924. Under the successors of Muck —Henri Rabaud and Pierre Monteux—the orchestra had deteriorated. The effects of the strike had not worn off when Koussevitzky took over. But Koussevitzky had ability and energy. His reputation marked him as one of the ablest of European conductors. He immediately set about reorganizing the symphony.

Older players were pensioned or released and some of the younger ones who were hired as replacements during the strike, but were only second-raters, were dismissed. The dismissal plan aroused some resentment among the players and there were new moves to affiliate with the union during 1925 and 1926. But efforts to unionize failed because the number of men who were sufficiently bold to show that they desired to join the union was too few. For more than 12 years thereafter attempts to unionize the orchestra were of negligible importance.

Europe was scoured for talent during the years succeeding 1924. The conductor felt that the best recruits were to be found there. But as the seasons passed, Koussevitzky became one of the more ardent exponents of American music. He also recognized the improved quality of American musical education and during the 1930's began engaging American-born musicians. It is true that the American Federation of Musicians blacklisted the members of the Boston Symphony and fined union members for playing at Koussevitzky's auditions. Nevertheless, many musicians went to the yearly auditions. When the second World War opened in 1939, the orchestra was largely American because of the new hiring policy and because most of the foreign-born players had been Americanized.

During the first 15 years of his connection with the orchestra, Koussevitzky remained neutral with regard to union matters. He was not antiunion. In 1902 he had organized the first musicians union in Russia and later he belonged to a musicians union in Paris. But he was pleased with the nonunion status of his orchestra because it gave him freedom from union regulations and restrictions. However, he succeeded in inducing the trustees not to put into effect a salary cut during the depression after one had already been made and generally he protected the men from the interference of management.

Notwithstanding Koussevitzky's efforts on behalf of the members of his orchestra, the symphony player in Boston had an inferior economic position in comparison to other musicians performing similar duties. The weekly stipend was smaller in Boston and the men did not have the same regularity in hours which other symphony players had. Union men received additional pay for extra rehearsals and much higher fees when they made symphony recordings. Apologists for the nonunion Boston orchestra conceded that the weekly remuneration was smaller in Boston but claimed that the annual salary was greater because of more regular employment. These contentions were unwarranted for though the season of the symphony man in Boston may have been slightly longer as a result of extensions through "pops" and festival programs, these engagements did not counterbalance the much greater weekly remuneration received by the union men. However, the Boston men made no move towards union affiliation.

Unionization of the Boston Symphony came from the outside. The orchestra's main income was derived from performances on the radio, for recording, and in the concert hall. Whatever deficit remained after the funds from these sources were exhausted was covered by contributions of the trustees and friends of the symphony. Shortly before 1940 the union undertook to make the deficit grow to a point where the financial burdens of the trustees would became impossible to bear. Petrillo was successful in carrying out this policy.

It was only two weeks after his elevation to the presidency of the national organization, that Petrillo began an intensive campaign to unionize the Boston Symphony Orchestra. The orchestra was one of the more important recorders for RCA Victor and control over the activities of the orchestra was necessary in order for Petrillo to be able to halt the production of all phonographic recordings and transcriptions. Some action had already been taken against the Boston orchestra in 1939 by the AFM. When the American Society of Composers, Authors and Publishers decided to sponsor a music festival in New York's Carnegie Hall, the Federation opposed the inclusion of the Boston Symphony in the recital. Fiorello H. La Guardia, mayor of New York, decided to remove the orchestra from the program and the New York Philharmonic Symphony Orchestra was substituted. In addition, the musicians union had prevented the Boston Symphony from performing over the radio subsequent to the 1938 season. The union had threatened to pull out its own musicians from radio programs if the broadcasters permitted the nonunion group to go on the air.

Although Petrillo was negotiating with the orchestra from the outset, he was neither in a vacillating mood, nor was he inclined to waver from a firm resolve to unionize the symphony. In August 1940 he told newspaper reporters: "They're through. We've taken them off the radio and off the records."[12] All record companies who desired to employ union musicians had been forced to secure licenses from the AFM. When the AFM ordered the RCA Victor company to stop recording the Boston Symphony or else suffer the loss of its license, the company hastened to obey. RCA Victor refused to renew its contract with the Boston orchestra. Pressed records of the orchestra, however, were released for many months thereafter because of the accumulated recordings cut prior to the termination of the agreement.

The strategy and tactics of the union with respect to the Boston Symphony may be divided into four parts. First, it involved removing the orchestra from radio programs. Secondly, the orchestra was prevented from making any recordings. These objectives were accomplished with promptness and dispatch and helped the union to isolate and cut off the orchestra financially.

Thirdly, Petrillo refused to grant solo instrumentalists and conductors permission to perform with the nonunion symphony orchestra. Violinists Efrem Zimbalist and Joseph Szigeti were refused permission to play scheduled dates. These men had joined the AFM after resigning from AGMA. Conductors Howard Hanson, Bruno Walter, and Carlos Chavez were similarly barred from conducting the Boston Symphony. Walter was an honorary member of the union and Chavez, as a Mexican alien, was the holder of a permit entitling him to lead union orchestras. The Boston orchestra was unable to obtain artists. (At the same time union policy barred nonunion conductors from leading union orchestras, although upon the personal appeal of Marshall Field 3d, president of the New York Philharmonic's board of directors, Petrillo consented to permit Koussevitzky to conduct a series of the New York society's concerts early in 1942.) The link between the enrollment of solo instrumentalists in the union and the unionization of the Boston Symphony Orchestra thus was made evident. The unionized solo instrumentalists and the unionized conductors could be prevented from accepting guest engagements with a nonunion orchestra.

The fourth action of the union was aimed at blocking the road tours of the orchestra. Concert halls which scheduled recitals by the Boston Symphony were told that they would be put on the union blacklist. This pressure was applied when the orchestra tried to use the municipal auditorium in Springfield, Massachusetts, the Eastman Theater in Rochester, New York, and Smith College in Northampton, Massachusetts. Though the union was not successful in securing the elimination of the orchestra from all of these halls, the orchestra undoubtedly suffered from some unfavorable publicity. The union also considered picketing Symphony Hall, home of the Boston orchestra. Carnegie Hall in New York City was put on the local's unfair list in June 1942 because it refused to agree to schedule only union orchestras. Petrillo, however, removed it from the list pending the outcome of his negotiations with the Boston Symphony. These negotiations already were on their way to successful termination.

Even as the union was tightening its vise-like grip on the orchestra, conferences between the AFM and the Boston Symphony had continued. As events unfolded, the executives of the Boston orchestra maintained strict silence on the matter of unionization. Only once was this rule broken. Rumors had persisted that the will of Henry L. Higginson had provided resources to the orchestra contingent upon its remaining free from unionism. George Judd, manager of the orchestra, emphatically stated that the will did not prohibit the employment of union musicians. In April 1942 Ernest B. Dane, president of the board of trustees of the orchestra, died. He had been resolute in his opposition to the union and, as the largest contributor, had been the orchestra's most influential policy maker. His death weakened opposition to the union. It then became possible for the parties to reach general agreement, although many details remained to be worked out subsequently.

Koussevitzky had been trying to get the trustees to permit unionization since 1939. He perceived the need for an uninterrupted flow of revenues from radio performances and recordings and he knew that the orchestra would suffer from its inability to obtain guest artists and interchange conductors. But he could not convince the trustees and he almost decided to sever his connection with the Boston group and come to New York as conductor of the Philharmonic. Petrillo appreciated the position of Koussevitzky and told a reporter: "Look here, the Boston Symphony wants the privilege of walking around the country as a nonunion organization, whereas 95 per cent of its members want to join. This includes Koussevitzky himself. How do I know? He told me so personally, when I visited him at his home in the Berkshires last summer." Petrillo added that Koussevitzky had advised him to "go easy" with the trustees. Petrillo then concluded: "I've been going easy for a year. But what do I get? A letter from Ernest B. Dane that he will stand by Judd as manager. And what did Judd write before that? He said he could not go over the head of the trustees. All right, if a fight is what they want, they can have it."[13]

In November 1942 the parties reached full agreement and a contract was signed. The 111 members of the Boston Symphony Orchestra, including the conductor and assistant conductors, agreed to join the union on condition that the orchestra be given the right to hire instrumentalists from any part of the United States and not, as had previously been required, only from within the jurisdiction of the local in which the orchestra was located. In order to effect this basic change, the laws of the union had to be modified. Petrillo consulted with representatives of 15 of the largest locals in the United States; the necessary revision of the union laws would directly affect these jurisdictions. As might be expected, the changes proposed by Petrillo were approved unanimously. Then under article I, section 1, of the bylaws of the union, Petrillo modified the bylaws to provide that all symphony orchestras might recruit players from any part of the United States. A symphony instrumentalist may now accept a symphony job in another jurisdiction without the permission of the local in whose jurisdiction the job is located.

These changes produced pleasant relations between the orchestra and the union. Although the repealed provisions concerning the employment of symphony players had not been enforced strictly and many exceptions had been permitted by the union, the trustees of the Boston orchestra felt that the mere existence of the restriction in the union law was a threat to the artistic integrity of the symphony. Said Serge Koussevitzky of Petrillo: "He's a very able man in his line. For his union he did a splendid job."[14] And indeed he did. But the time element had favored Petrillo and had played a leading role in breaking down the resistance of the directors of the orchestra to the union.

After 61 years of opposition to unionization, the Boston Symphony Orchestra was forced to yield. The immediate cause of its capitulation was dire financial necessity. Though this orchestra was one of the world's finest and had been run efficiently and economically, its budget could not be balanced. In some cities, deficits were paid from the contributions of a few patrons of art. In Boston, Higginson had made up the difference between the income and outlay of the orchestra, and had at the same time dictated the policies. After his death this task was taken up by others. When Dane died, no person or group of persons was willing to meet the deficit from its own resources. The income that could be derived from radio engagements, recordings, and road tours became indispensable for the continued solvency of the orchestra.

Freedom in the selection of orchestra members had become a changed problem over the years. The first decades of the century had been highlighted by union attempts to prevent the influx of foreign musicians into this country. Orchestras and bands, however, operated on the assumption that foreign players generally surpassed American instrumentalists. The union took a long-range point of view and stressed the need for improving the opportunities of American musicians and making more adequate use of their talent. Laws restricting alien contract labor were only partially successful from the union's point of view, but immigration restrictions were somewhat more effective. The first World War helped the union by cutting off the supply of immigrants. In some cases the contract labor law had an indirect influence on the number of foreign musicians entering the United States. When a musician from abroad was brought to this country in the expectation of subsequently getting a contract from the Boston Symphony, he had to wait several months in order to meet the requirements of the law. As a result the musician insisted that the contract which he finally signed should include special provisions and should be of long duration. This arrangement made for more rigid conditions and reduced the flexibility of the orchestra.

The sound musical training instituted by American high schools, colleges, and music schools had improved the quality of orchestra players here. The foresight and vision of Koussevitzky in substituting American men for the older foreign players in the orchestra had eliminated a major grievance of the union. In 1918, the Boston Symphony Orchestra consisted of 100 men. Of these, 51 were American citizens but only 17 were native born. Twenty-two were German, eight Austrian, six Dutch, three French, two British, two Italian, two Russian, two Belgian, and two Bohemians. In 1940 native Americans dominated the orchestra.

The Boston Symphony Orchestra, therefore, was more inclined to deal with the union. Money derived from recordings and radio programs was essential for the continuation of operations. In order to obtain such funds the demands of the union had to be met. But it was now possible for the orchestra to recruit an adequate supply of excellent musicians by sifting the United States, because American players had attained extreme proficiency and were among the best in the world. As soon as the union was ready to make a few concessions the basis for an agreement was found. The long struggle ended with a complete understanding when the union consented to modify its hiring requirements. The importance of nonunion musicians in the United States was entirely eliminated and the union's control over professional musicians became complete.

Petrillo had accomplished his preliminary tasks. The two weaknesses in the organization of musicians which he had found when he became president were eliminated. The solo instrumentalists had been taken away from the American Guild of Musical Artists and the Boston Symphony had been converted into a union orchestra. His fight with the record companies now could be undertaken.

> "[The companies resorted to] bitterness, injustice, trick-
> ery and reactionism which would do justice to slave-
> owners [; they engaged in a] vile, indecent, malicious
> and filthy campaign of libel, slander and vilification. . . .
> Honesty and fairness . . . triumphed over falsity and
> fraud. . . . If . . . the companies, fail to change [their
> past course], the A.F.M. will not hesitate to break off
> relations and leave them to die by their own nefarious
> schemes."
>
> JAMES CAESAR PETRILLO

• The Cessation of Recording

Petrillo realized that the ban on the production of recordings
which he had imposed on Chicago musicians for 18 months in
1937 and 1938 had cost the members of his local a quarter of a
million dollars in wages. Yet he was not afraid to re-engage in
battle against mechanical music. The conventions of 1941 and
1942 had authorized him to try to bring to an end the production of musical records and transcriptions. When Petrillo had
succeeded in his preliminary maneuvers and had brought all
instrumentalists into the union, he acted with dispatch.

Late in June 1942, the recording and transcription companies
were notified that after August 1, members of the AFM would
not play or contract to make records, transcriptions, or other
types of mechanical reproduction of music. Elmer Davis, director
of the Office of War Information, requested the union to withdraw its notices, but he was turned down; the order went into
effect as scheduled. Senator Burton K. Wheeler's offer to mediate
between the union and the companies was rejected by the union
on the grounds that it had no intention of dealing or negotiating with the companies.

Meanwhile, however, the government had intervened in the
record controversy in two ways. In August, Senator D. Worth
Clark introduced a resolution in Congress to investigate Pe-

trillo and the union. Preliminary hearings were held and the resolution was approved.[1] In January 1943, Petrillo and his counsel appeared before the subcommittee of the Senate Committee on Interstate Commerce which was inquiring into the ban on records. After lengthy testimony Petrillo promised to negotiate with the companies. The government also acted through the Department of Justice. In July 1942, Attorney General Francis Biddle authorized Thurman Arnold of the Department of Justice to seek an injunction from the United States District Court to prevent the union from engaging in restraint of trade and from violating the Sherman Antitrust Act. The judge, however, supported the contention of the union that a labor dispute was involved and he therefore did not issue any injunction. The United States Supreme Court upheld the decision of the lower court.[2] A second suit to secure an injunction was dropped by the Department of Justice in April 1943 after Tom C. Clark replaced Arnold as Assistant Attorney General.

For six months Petrillo held firm to his resolution not to permit his members to make musical recordings. He had told the 1942 convention of the union that the industry would be permitted to produce records if it gave assurances that they would be used only in the home or that they would be used by the armed forces; the ban would be dropped if President Roosevelt would so request. During the first month after recording had ceased, the manufacture of transcriptions which were to be used only once and then destroyed had been permitted by Petrillo. He had canceled this authorization when his lawyers advised him that the concession might be construed as a violation of the law because it discriminated in favor of commercial transcriptions and against library recordings and phonographic records. The position of the union in the recording controversy was supported by various groups and persons, mainly labor organizations. In October 1942 the convention of the American Federation of Labor, upon the recommendation of its executive council, passed a resolution approving the ban on records.

The Puerto Rico Federation of Musicians announced that it was supporting the AFM and that it too was banning the production of musical recordings. The Puerto Rican musicians claimed that this position was also being taken by the musicians of Cuba and Argentina. The Musicians Union of Great Britain pledged itself to aid the AFM by preventing the export of musical records from Great Britain. The British musicians did not resume making records for shipment to the United States and Canada, until after the AFM had reached an agreement with the recording companies. This was of vital importance to Petrillo for it eliminated what might have become a means of dissipating the effectiveness of the ban on production which had been imposed in the United States. Members of the AFM backed the ban and completely refrained from making recordings. Personnel of name bands and symphony orchestras and solo instrumentalists who were unable to record and whose incomes were therefore curtailed, voiced very few complaints.

External opposition to the action taken by the union was more vociferous and bitter. The public was disquieted. A Gallup poll at the end of the summer of 1942 showed that 73 per cent of the people favored legal action by the government to stop Petrillo, while only 12 per cent were opposed. The chief antagonism to the union and Petrillo came from the National Association of Broadcasters. The NAB is the trade association of the radio industry; and although it has enrolled most of the stations in the country among its membership, it is dominated by the large networks. In 1943, James L. Fly, then chairman of the Federal Communications Commission characterized the NAB as a "stooge organization" before a Senate committee. The Association was vociferous in denouncing, taunting, and reviling Petrillo. Acrimonious speeches were made, disparaging pamphlets were issued, special bulletins were published, and cartoons ridiculing Petrillo were reproduced. The dictatorial implications of Petrillo's middle name—Caesar—were stressed by the NAB; Petrillo complained that the NAB had spent a million and a half dollars publicizing this fact. Petrillo undoubtedly did not know that in 1908, the American Federation of Musicians had attacked the policies recommended by the temporary chairman of the Republican national convention, Julius Caesar Burroughs; the AFM emphasized that such proposals might be expected from a person bearing the names "Julius Caesar."[3]

The campaign waged by the NAB against the policy of the musicians union was reinforced by the specific employers affected

—the recording companies and the radio broadcasters. The recording industry consists of two parts. Some companies manufacture records and others manufacture electrical transcriptions. Phonographic records are readily available to the public. About 80 per cent of the records are purchased for use in the home, 19 per cent are bought for use in juke boxes located in hotels, restaurants, and dance halls, and one per cent is obtained by radio stations. The bulk of the records made in the United States are produced by six companies—Columbia Recording Corporation (affiliated with CBS), RCA Victor (affiliated with NBC), Decca Records, Capitol Records, Mercury Record Corporation, and MGM Records.

Electrical transcriptions are specially prepared 33-inch platters which, because of the materials utilized and the method of recording, may be used only for radio broadcasts. The transcription business has two distinct divisions, generally known as library and commercial. Library transcriptions are rented by stations for use on sustaining programs—that is, programs which have no commercial sponsor. Like phonograph records, they may be played many times. Commercial transcriptions record broadcasts which are sponsored by advertisers. They are rarely used more than once. The radio recording division of NBC controls a very large proportion of the transcription business. Only a handful of firms render library service, though there are a larger number engaged in making commercial transcriptions. The gross annual income of the transcription industry amounts to several million dollars.

The closed shop has prevailed in the recording industry for many years, but until 1944 no negotiations concerning working conditions ever took place. The AFM laid down the terms, including the amount of wages to be paid and the number of hours to be worked, and the companies adopted them. The original reason for licensing the recording companies in 1938 was to force them to restrict the use of records to noncommercial purposes. The court subsequently determined that such a limitation could not be enforced legally.[4] Nevertheless the union continued to issue licenses until the recording ban went into effect.

The interests of the radio broadcasting companies have been intertwined with those of the recording companies. Senator

Burton K. Wheeler had at one time been advised by Petrillo to investigate this connection, but Wheeler had been persuaded by the radio interests not to do so. Radio stations and networks were strongly opposed to the record ban. Most of the newspapers in the country supported the radio industry but this attitude at least partially depended on the fact that many of them own or control radio stations.

Petrillo stressed that he could not expect very much more employment from the recording companies, and that he was really interested in getting at the radio stations. Nearly 75 per cent of all radio time has been devoted to music; less than half has consisted of live music and the remainder has constituted recorded programs. The proportions have varied among the stations, the amount of recorded music having been much smaller, in general, on network outlets. Though the AFM conceded that at least half of the radio stations earned incomes which were too small to enable them to hire live musicians, it demanded that stations which could afford to do so, should increase the number of staff musicians. The union claimed that musicians should share in the huge profits of the radio industry.

Bargaining with radio networks has been carried on mainly on a local basis and handled by the local unions, but the national organization has always been ready to help the local deal with a station that is part of a network system. The AFM was formerly able to do this by getting the network to induce the local station to accept the terms of the local union.

Petrillo made a good impression when he testified before a subcommittee of the Senate Committee on Interstate Commerce on January 12 and 13, 1943.[5] He stated that the union was willing to negotiate with the recording industry in order to work out a just solution. At one point Senator Clark broke into the discussion and said to Petrillo: "Would you change jobs with one of us? Today I would," was the answer he received.[6]

In February 1943 the union proposed that recording companies should pay a fee for each record and transcription made by union members. These fees would be put into a fund to be used for the reduction of unemployment among musicians. Both the phonographic record companies and the transcription companies, which bargained separately with the union, turned the proposal down. The companies refused to make payments into a fund which would be used for the benefit of musicians whom they had never employed. After several months of fruitless conferences, the negotiations lapsed. Some of the companies affected appealed to the United States Conciliation Service, and when this agency could not settle the dispute it certified the matter to the National War Labor Board.

Many of the companies, however, were in no haste to settle the issues. Radio stations and juke box operators had had long notice of Petrillo's intention to ban recording, and they had accumulated huge stocks of musical selections. The recorders continued to release records by pressing reissues and by dipping into the backlogs which they had built up. They also manufactured records and transcriptions for the United States government. Petrillo permitted musicians to make recordings in connection with the government's war effort.

The companies continued to record vocal arrangements, but when they attempted to use vocal backgrounds simulating music, Petrillo felt that they were going too far. He warned the top ranking singers against this practice. They agreed to refrain from using such backgrounds when they were told that the musicians union would eventually take account of all their activities during the ban. Recordings of music with instruments not then covered by the union rules or contracts—such as harmonicas, ocarinas, and one-man bands—continued to be made but they found little popular appeal. "Bootleg" recordings carrying names like Hal Goodman, Peter Piper, and Johnny Jones, were made to circumvent the ban, but they were not numerous. Other records were brought in from Mexico and Cuba.

There was another reason why the record ban applied by Petrillo was not too burdensome on industry. The record manufacturers were faced by an acute shortage of raw materials. India has been the only source of supply of shellac and little of this substance was imported during the war. Shellac normally constitutes 20 per cent of the matter in each disk. It is used because it pours evenly when the record is pressed, it resists heat when the record is played, and it keeps surface noise down. The only satisfactory substitute for shellac is vinylite (used in making transcriptions) but the high cost has made it uneconomical to use vinylite in the production of records. Manufacturers, thus dependent on reprocessed and salvaged shellac, found that production costs had increased and that the quality of the records had been reduced. This situation and the imposition of quotas by the government limiting the amount of virgin shellac which the record companies could consume were responsible for a decrease in the output of records.

As a result the recording industry had time to consider what to do and to delay the acceptance of proposals submitted. When the case went to the NWLB, the AFM denied that that agency had any jurisdiction. In spite of the fact that the union had maintained, and succeeded in winning its case before the courts on grounds that it was involved in a labor dispute with the recording companies, it denied to the NWLB that any labor controversy existed. The American Federation of Musicians therefore claimed that the NWLB had no jurisdiction. Following a short hearing, however, the NWLB assumed jurisdiction of the case in July 1943.

After the Board panel had begun hearings, Decca Records capitulated to the union demands and signed an agreement in September. Gradually all of the other record and transcription companies accepted similar terms and they also signed contracts. But Columbia, RCA Victor, and the NBC transcription division refused to agree to the principle of making payments to the union and continued the case before the panel. In March 1944, the panel recommended to the NWLB that the men should be ordered back to work and that no royalty plan should be approved. In June, the NWLB handed down its decision.[7] The Board decided that the musicians should return to work at once, but overruled the panel and held that immediate negotiations should be held regarding the amount of contributions that employers should make to a welfare fund.

The union, however, rejected the Board's directive. It refused to work for the three companies unless they accepted contracts similar to those agreed to by the others. The companies refused to comply with the union's demand and the NWLB turned the case over to Fred M. Vinson, Director of Economic Stabilization. The union argued that war agencies had no jurisdiction over the matter because the war effort was not involved; despite the fact that Chauncey A. Weaver, a member of the union's international executive board for many years had maintained, in another connection, that music is a war essential.

Nevertheless, neither Vinson nor James F. Byrnes, Director of War Mobilization was able to settle the case and it was referred to President Roosevelt. On October 4, 1944, Roosevelt sent a telegram to Petrillo asking him to comply with the NWLB directive. Roosevelt said that he would not seize the industry because noncompliance by the union was not unduly impeding the war effort, but that he hoped the union would accept the decision in the interests of orderly government.

Although Petrillo had stated publicly that he would end the record ban if requested to do so by President Roosevelt, his statement had been made before *any* of the companies had signed agreements. Since almost all of them had come to terms by October 1944, Petrillo turned down the request of the president. He refused to give advantageous terms to those companies which had not yet signed. Roosevelt announced that he would check the law to see what he could do about Petrillo's decision. But the president did nothing further and many people were disappointed by his failure to act. The disappointment, in one instance, was expressed the following year during hearings held by a committee of the House of Representatives. Paul A. Porter, chairman of the Federal Communications Commission, was testifying. The dialogue was: *"Mr. Brown.* Do you mean to say that even the appeal of the President did not move Mr. Petrillo in the stand he had taken with reference to those records? *Mr. Porter.* Mr. Petrillo was adamant. *Mr. Brown.* What was that word? *Mr. Porter.* Mr. Petrillo did not budge. *Mr. Brown.* You mean he just did not budge. *Mr. Porter.* That is right. *Mr. Brown.* And there wasn't anybody who carried him out of his office, was there? *Mr. Porter.* No."[8]

Columbia and RCA Victor were not able to procrastinate any longer because their competitive positions were deteriorating rapidly. The War Production Board had increased shellac quotas substantially and the output of records had begun to rise. Decca, some of whose album sales reached enormous proportions, was recording almost all the new tunes (a few smaller and newer companies were expanding under the unusually auspicious conditions). But more important in prompting the decision of Columbia and RCA Victor was the possibility that many of their artists would switch to Decca. The imminence of such changes was demonstrated when Jascha Heifetz ended his long exclusive connection with RCA Victor and signed a non-exclusive agreement with Decca.

Although Columbia and RCA Victor had hesitated to concede the principle of paying royalties to the union because it might have led to similar demands by the union on the parent radio networks, they were constrained to acquiesce by circumstances. In November 1944, they agreed to terms and the bitter dispute ended. It had lasted more than 27 months. Said Petrillo after it was over: "[The companies resorted to] bitterness, injustice, trickery and reactionism which would do justice to slaveowners [; they engaged in a] vile, indecent, malicious and filthy campaign of libel, slander and vilification. . . . Honesty and fairness . . . triumphed over falsity and fraud. . . . If . . . the companies, fail to change [their past course], the A.F.M. will not hesitate to break off relations and leave them to die by their own nefarious schemes." When Petrillo was asked to comment on the companies' statement that the government was either unwilling or unable to enforce its orders, he said: "Why should I? I've already called them every goddamned name I could think of."9

The contracts signed by Columbia and RCA Victor were similar to those of the other companies except that provisions were added that should the union call a strike against either of them, then their artists would be free to work for any recording companies not involved in the dispute. The major provisions of these contracts, which eventually applied to about 600 companies, established a fund controlled by the union into which the companies paid a specified sum of money for every record and transcription produced with the services of musicians. The fees paid for each record varied from a quarter of a cent for 35 cent disks to five cents for two-dollar records; and the fee was two and a half per cent of the selling price of those records which sold for more than two dollars. No fee was paid for commercial electrical transcriptions manufactured for a single broadcast but library transcriptions were assessed a sum amounting to three per cent of the gross revenues derived from their use. The union was given access to the books of the companies and the companies were required to obtain permission from the union to record any studio broadcasts. When rebroadcasting transcriptions, the companies agreed to pay scale wages to the musicians who had made the recording. All contracts were arranged to terminate on December 31, 1947.

These contracts represented a milestone in labor relations. They were the first major contractual arrangements of the post-war period under which employers paid money directly to a labor organization and the agreements marked the beginning of the establishment of a large number of welfare funds. Most of the recording contracts specified that the purpose of the fund was to foster musical culture by employing live musicians and that no more than five per cent of the moneys collected could be used for administration. The contracts stipulated that wage scales could be changed only once during the period in which the agreement applied. The union did not gain any direct control over wired music or juke boxes (including telephone music boxes in which patrons choose the selection through a telephone device; and "soundies" in which the music boxes have a picture accompaniment).

In October 1946, the wage provisions of the contract were re-examined and Petrillo was able to secure wage increases of 37½ per cent for recording services and of 50 per cent for transcription work. The new base was $41.25 for three hours of regular recording or $38.50 for two hours of recording by symphony orchestras. Services of musicians for electrical transcriptions were fixed at $27 for 15 minutes.

● *Union Activities during the Second World War*

Despite the union's ban on recordings and transcriptions, it contributed generously and patriotically to the nation's war effort. The government generally paid for services rendered to it during the war, but the musicians contributed millions of dollars worth of free music to different government agencies and to army camps and hospitals. The union offered the services of its members without charge to the army and navy so that the armed forces could make records and transcriptions. Union members even played for RCA Victor and Columbia during the period when the recording case was before the NWLB.

The musicians union reintroduced some of the policies it had followed during the first World War. By an order of Petrillo, it exempted all members of the union who enlisted in the armed forces, from the payment of dues and assessments. It required bands and orchestras to play the Star Spangled Banner at the beginning and end of each concert or musical program. It purchased many thousands of dollars of United States and Canadian war bonds. It fought to raise the rank of the army band leader from warrant officer to commissioned status.

Late in 1942, Petrillo visited President Roosevelt at the White House. At Roosevelt's suggestion, the AFM undertook to present a program of free public concerts in the smaller communities of the nation. In the summer of the following year the union completed its plans. The most important symphonic orchestras in the country agreed to take part. Although the AFM had admitted that recordings by symphony orchestras did not displace live musicians and although the leading orchestras had requested the union to remove the ban because much of their income had been derived from recording work, the orchestras agreed to cooperate in the project to spread symphonic music even though they had received no relief. Nearly 80 concerts were played by 20 leading symphony orchestras. All expenses, including the payment of more than $100,000 in wages to the members of the orchestras, were borne by the AFM. Transportation difficulties forced the cancellation of many scheduled concerts. The concerts met with general acclaim though some opposition to them was expressed by members of the union who believed that the money should have been spent to help unemployed musicians rather than to employ symphony instrumentalists—a group already receiving high wages.

● *Problems related to the Radio Industry*

The union gained an impressive victory when it negotiated the establishment of the employment fund but simultaneously it abandoned one of its major objectives. The union had not opposed making records for home use, but it had contended that radio stations should not be permitted to use phonographic records. In spite of the opinion of the panel of the National War Labor Board that radio broadcasting had not displaced live music, the union maintained that such was the case. It argued that stations were making excessive use of records. The union was pleased with the action of the Canadian government which prohibited the use of recordings on radio stations in the

Dominion during evening hours; since this regulation encouraged the use of live talent.

The union particularly objected to the activities of certain disk jockeys who were making large sums of money from musical records but were not paying anything to musicians. During the period when the record ban was in effect, the union engaged in a brief strike at station WNEW in New York City because Martin Block, disk jockey of the "Make Believe Ballroom" program, played recordings of American tunes imported from Great Britain. These records had been shipped to him by a friend in England, though normally the British musicians union had had to give written consent before any records could be exported. Further controversy was averted when Block agreed to stop using such records. WNEW had provided very little employment for musicians, yet had been grossing over a million dollars each year. A small station, WINX in Washington, D. C., increased its value tenfold in four years by selling advertisements on its musically recorded programs.

The radio stations were not affected by the terms of the settlement between the union and the record companies since the price of records did not rise. But the AFM continued trying to get the radio stations to employ more musicians. The locals in the union have had the major responsibility for the achievement of this task although the AFM has helped them with all possible means. The AFM itself has been mainly concerned in the negotiations with the four major networks. Since almost all network programs originate in New York, Los Angeles, and Chicago, the locals in these three cities have had the major role in negotiating. Generally the locals have worked out wage scales with the networks, and the AFM has been chiefly concerned with working conditions. Since April 1946, however, all network broadcasting contract provisions for musicians, other than for staff orchestras and staff leaders, have had to be approved by the AFM. Local contracts usually have run for three years, but negotiations scheduled in 1947 were postponed to 1948 by extending the contracts then in force.

Like other unions, the AFM has tried to secure guaranteed employment for its members. The AFM, therefore, has tried to get radio stations to use a greater number of permanent staff musicians. Although there have been over 2,100 licenses issued to standard or AM broadcasting stations by the Federal Communications Commission in the United States, only 301 of them employed musicians steadily throughout the year in 1949. One hundred and one additional stations used musicians with some regularity. Forty-nine others employed musicians on a single engagement basis only. Two hundred and fifty-nine of these stations employing musicians were affiliated with networks and 192 were independent. Steady staff employment accounted for the jobs of 2,450 musicians who received ten and three-quarter million dollars during the year. Single engagement broadcasting for sustaining programs provided musicians with a little over two and a quarter million dollars, distributed among several thousand men.[10] Single engagement commercial broadcasting employment in the United States that year provided jobs for about 3,700 men and yielded an income of over five and a third million dollars. Since 1949, except for network staff musicians, there has been a further decline in radio employment.

The union attempted to increase radio employment in various ways. The technique which evoked the greatest criticism was the requirement of standbys. Standby musicians formerly had to be used by radio stations when programs were put on which included amateurs, nonunion musicians, or traveling musicians from other jurisdictions. This practice prevailed until the passage of the Lea Act in 1946. For example, the union required the employment of a standby band of union musicians when a naval band broadcast at the graduation exercises of the Great Lakes Naval Training Station in 1942. (In making a film, the the Canadian government had to pay the AFM a standby fee of $60 in 1946 because it used a nonunion church organist.)

For several years the union was perplexed by the problem arising from remote control programs. Music played by name bands at hotels, restaurants, and night clubs was piped over the air by radio stations. Booking agents who controlled radio lines were able to select the bands that played over the air. The union maintained that this procedure limited competition among orchestras and unfairly reduced the opportunities of some bands to play on the radio. The AFM, however, was able to get the radio stations, for a time, to pay the bands additional remuneration when the music was picked up and in 1940 executed an agreement with the stations by which all radio lines were removed from the control of bookers. Radio lines have been handled since by the stations themselves. Today, stations announce that remote control programs are broadcast through the courtesy of James C. Petrillo and the American Federation of Musicians. The AFM expects that such pickups will not replace programs which would have employed live musicians.

In 1941 the union suddenly banned musicians from playing on cooperatively sponsored programs. These network programs are broadcast across the country, but each region has a different sponsor. The union maintained that sponsors were not paying for the full value of the services rendered by the musicians. The union claimed that it was losing employment opportunities because cooperative programs eliminated the need for local concerns to advertise on local programs and to employ live musicians; and that such programs arranged by a national network threw many local bands out of work. Naturally, radio stations were reluctant to pay standby fees, although the AFM never made such requests. For a considerable period of time, cooperatively sponsored programs were not permitted to use musicians. Instead they substituted vocal choirs for musicians. Some of the programs affected were the Joan Davis show, Meet Me at Parky's, Abbott and Costello, Alexander's Mediation Board, and Headline Edition. Information Please, which previously had had a single sponsor, became a cooperative program in 1947. Since the show had depended partly upon the performance of a pianist and was no longer able to use one, the producer filed charges with the National Labor Relations Board. He claimed that the union violated the Taft-Hartley Act by denying musicians to Information Please and by engaging in an illegal boycott against the program. Although the union contract was with the networks, Petrillo, upon their advice, removed the ban in November 1947. The immediate effect was that several cooperative programs engaged the services of orchestras and individual musicians. Petrillo, however, undertook to determine the long-run effects of his action.

The action of the union in prohibiting the networks from broadcasting any musical programs emanating from foreign countries other than Canada was of wider significance. This rule had been in effect prior to the war, but it was waived by the union during wartime to promote goodwill with other nations. It was reinstituted after the war ended. The union maintained that musical programs coming in from foreign countries tended to reduce the employment opportunities of American musicians. It argued that government policy prohibited the importation of contract labor musicians to prevent competition with American musicians and that the broadcasting of foreign music was an evasion of the intent of Congress. The AFM did not want such music to be broadcast in the United States.

Only a few stations were affected by the ban but the protests were numerous. The action by the union was considered a setback to the cultural program of the United Nations. Petrillo assured some of his critics that the ban on foreign music in no way limited the broadcast of special religious services. Although the Lea Act prohibited the union from continuing to impose such restrictions, the AFM nevertheless has apparently had an oral understanding with the networks that music originating in foreign countries, in general, will not be rebroadcast in or relayed to the United States.

The general prohibition against the employment of foreign musicians in the United States was enforced rigidly. Cuban consular officials threatened diplomatic action to break the ban. The Mexican musicians union temporarily banned United States musicians in retaliation. The British musicians union, however, generally has supported Petrillo's actions. Petrillo had also required American broadcasting companies to secure the permission of the union before sending musical programs outside of the United States and Canada.

• The Recording and Transcription Fund

As union collections from the recording and transcription companies increased criticism simultaneously began to mount. Though the union had stated many times that the fund would be used only to employ musicians without jobs, many persons remained skeptical. Opposition voices became even louder when John L. Lewis won a welfare fund for the miners in the coal industry. Critics feared that the royalty principle would be extended to labor contracts in general. The AFM was not able to convince the public that the two funds were basically different. The musicians maintained that the miners were producing a commodity which was consumed after being used once and that therefore they were not digging themselves out of jobs. Musicians, however, were making records which could be played over many times and thus they were helping to displace themselves.

In February 1947, the AFM put into effect a plan for the expenditure of the recording fund which had been worked out at the end of 1946 by Petrillo and a committee of three local union presidents. As was anticipated by those who were familiar with the sincere intentions of the leaders of the union, the fund was allocated for the employment of musicians. During the first allocation, each local, except the three largest, was entitled to receive $10.43 for each member in good standing. The largest three locals were entitled to this sum for each of their first 5,000 members and to $2.00 for each additional member. Every program planned by any local had to be approved by the national union.

Locals employed their own members to give the free public concerts. Though the national union attempted to regulate the locals strictly and ordered that no part of the allocated money could be used for administrative purposes, complaints were expressed by many members. There were charges leveled against some locals that favoritism helped particular musicians to secure employment and that the unemployed were not necessarily the ones hired. Many of these charges, however, were aired by disgruntled members.

Royalties paid to the musicians union during the life of the contract were substantial. Almost all of this money came from the recording, not transcription, companies. The sums paid to the union kept increasing each year because the output of new records kept rising; because the relative sale of more expensive records, on which the royalties were higher, rose; and because payments were made on new pressings of recordings made in previous years covered by the agreement.

The money in the recording and transcription fund was collected in a period of slightly more than four years—from the signing of the contracts in 1943 to the end of 1947—although small sums were received later because some of the records made under the contracts were sold subsequently. During those years, the record and transcription companies contributed more than $4,500,000 to the fund. Almost all of this money was spent by the union in the three years between 1947 and 1950. It gave nearly 19,000 performances at veterans hospitals, public schools, and other institutions. The types of performances in order of frequency included teen-age dances, entertaining units, band concerts, orchestra concerts, regular dances, jazz concerts, parades, and symphony concerts. More than 450,00 jobs for single engagements were made available. These income and expenditure figures are not connected with the music performance trust fund set up by the union in 1948.

The most publicized free concert given by the AFM under the program was the one held in Washington, D. C., on May 25, 1948. It was attended by President Harry S. Truman, many members of the Senate and the House of Representatives, and numerous other high government and labor officials. The affair was very successful. Subsequently, Petrillo was named National Music Chairman for the inauguration of Truman in 1948. On January 17, 1949, Petrillo gave President Truman, who plays the piano, a gold card making him an honorary member of the AFM for life. At the end of the presentation, which was also attended by William Green of the AFL, Petrillo and Green said to Truman: "We are now your presidents, just as you are our President."[11] On June 19, 1949, a recording and transcription concert was given at Colorado Springs, Colorado, in connection with the annual conference of governors.

Union policies generally were carried out with great success by the AFM. At the same time, a growing public interest in musical developments brought about greater public concern with the methods, tactics, and policies pursued by the union. The end of the war enabled Congress to focus more attention on the activities of this union.

"This fellow [Petrillo] has gone too far. We've got to clip his wings. But we don't want to interfere with the legitimate functions of a union."

CLARENCE J. BROWN

• Competition from Amateurs

If Petrillo had been content to confine his dispute with the radio networks to matters dealing with recordings and to the wages and hours of musicians employed by the stations, he might have succeeded completely in his objectives. The position taken by the musicians had substantial merit and impressed those conversant with the recording problem that the welfare fund was an equitable solution. The clamor of the National Association of Broadcasters was loud, and was echoed by large parts of the press and the public. Yet these vociferations would have subsided in due course. Petrillo's zest for protecting and improving the welfare of his members knew no bounds, however, and consequently he overreached himself and infuriated many Congressmen.

Petrillo had ascribed many of the hardships of the musicians to the radio industry and he felt that all aspects of the matter should be considered at one time. He decided that the ban on the production of records solved only one phase of the problem and that the competition between amateurs, especially school orchestras, and professional musicians for radio time must be eliminated. He probably did not realize that the achievement of this goal could be of only slight benefit to musicians. When amateur musicians played on the air standby fees usually were paid to the AFM; though no fees generally were paid when school bands were involved. Furthermore, the number of such programs was extremely limited. Petrillo's trait of ignoring the attitudes and opinions of the public when undertaking an action on behalf of the musicians was not sensible. In return for the little he could gain by taking school-boys off the radio, he became deeply involved in unfavorable publicity. Congress then passed restrictive labor legislation aimed at the musicians union which served as the harbinger of a more general law curtailing the power of unions.

The music of high school and college bands and orchestras for years had been one of the cultural features presented by radio stations. Young musicians have been encouraged and stimulated in pursuing their musical education by appearances on the radio. Petrillo recognized this fact and together with Mrs. Eleanor Roosevelt he had sponsored a National Youth Administration children's orchestra on the air. At the end of 1941, however, Petrillo was successful in forcing the cancellation of a number of broadcasts. These programs were scheduled as part of a series of presentations by the Music Educators National Conference. School bands in Chicago, Cleveland, Washington, Milwaukee, St. Louis, and San Francisco, among other cities, were not permitted to go on the air. And in New York City, only the intervention of Mayor La Guardia enabled a radio program to be scheduled at the High School of Music and Art. These isolated restrictions, however, aroused little attention.

During the middle of 1941, a more serious controversy began. Petrillo told the National Broadcasting Company that the summer series of concerts played by the National Music Camp at Interlochen, Michigan must not be permitted to go on the air. This camp had opened in 1928 as a summer music school and had been attended every year by boys and girls selected on a competitive basis from all over the United States. In 1930 it began a series of radio programs over NBC which continued through 1941. The manufacturers of Majestic Radios sponsored the concerts in 1930 and paid for a standby orchestra of union musicians. Each week that the program was on the air that year an announcement had been made stating that the broadcast was performed in cooperation with the American Federation of Musicians. From 1931 on, the program was a sustaining feature of the network and no standby musicians were employed.

When Petrillo made his demand of NBC in 1941, it was explained to him that all the contractual and other arrangements for the year had been completed, and that much inconvenience would result from any changes. The union leader then dropped his request on the understanding that the matter would be reopened by the company before scheduling the camp for the 1942 season. The company either ignored or violated this agreement with the union and completed plans for the 1942 Interlochen series. Just before the first concert was to go on the air in the second week in July, however, Petrillo ordered NBC to cancel the series. In a large measure the company had forced his hand. Petrillo had acted with moderation and though many persons felt that the 160 boys and girls of the school orchestra had been roughly treated, there was no other course of action which he could take. While the objective of the union in this case was not felicitous, the decision had not been made in haste.

The union had a closed shop agreement with the network which permitted only professional musicians be used on the radio. The AFM maintained that since the number of hours of radio broadcast time is fixed, the more hours that are allocated to the nonprofessional musicians—amateurs and school players— the less that remain for the professional. Petrillo pointed out that the Interlochen camp was a commercial enterprise because it charged the students tuition fees and that the radio concerts were used to advertise the camp and to attract new pupils. Actually, school instructors formed the nucleus of the broadcasting orchestra.

Dr. Joseph E. Maddy, the chief spokesman for the school, was the founder and president of the camp and a professor of music at the University of Michigan. The National Music Camp had become affiliated with the university in 1942. About 40 courses were given in the camp by the university and nearly 200 college students attended. Maddy claimed that the institution was not a commercial enterprise because the tuition fee of $300 for the eight-week period covered the cost of clothing, board, the use of instruments, library privileges, and camp facilities. He added that although tuition is charged by colleges and universities in the United States, they thereby do not become commercial enterprises. The National Music Camp had been granted tax exemption as a nonprofit educational institution, under opinions of the United States Attorney General and the Michigan Attorney General. Furthermore, beginning in 1939, each session of the Michigan legislature had made specific appropriations to the camp and guest conductors such as Frederick Stock and Walter Damrosch, had rendered their services without charge.

Many musicians associated with the Interlochen school had not joined the union. Representatives of the camp maintained that the average age of the children in the orchestra was 15 years and that they were therefore ineligible to become members of the union. But there were undoubtedly many who met the age requirements and who were not in the union. More than half of the 50 instructors were members of the American Federation of Musicians, Maddy himself having been a member in good standing ever since 1909. The camp authorities, who were joined by other educators, stated that the action by Petrillo discouraged the youths and hindered musical education, without benefiting professional musicians. They noted that NBC merely had substituted a studio symphony orchestra for the Interlochen concert without hiring any additional musicians. Maddy contended also that the refusal to allow the children to play over the air was similar to a requirement that motorists must join a taxi drivers union or that persons who delivered an address over the radio must join a union.

The American Federation of Musicians did not offer to negotiate or compromise on this issue. When information was requested of Petrillo regarding the Interlochen situation, he said: "Too many people are talking about it. Too many people know more about it than we do. So we'll let them settle it."[1] On other occasions when reporters were looking for him, the union chief was "out of town." From the union point of view, banning the school children from the air was an ill-conceived, ill-advised, and unfortunate step. Even assuming that some additional work might have been gained by professional musicians, though this result never was clearly evident, the benefit seemed scarcely worth the risk of arousing and antagonizing the public. This was especially true at a time when the recording ban had just been announced.

In July 1942, immediately after Petrillo's order to NBC, the Federal Communications Commission began an investigation of the Interlochen situation at the instigation of Senator Arthur H. Vandenberg of Michigan. In August, the Senate passed a resolution, already noted in connection with the ban on recordings, to investigate the musicians union, which contained a reference in its preamble to the matter of school orchestras. But these probes were ineffective. Nor were the appeals made to William Green of the AFL and to Vice President Henry A. Wallace to intervene of any avail. Instead, the Cincinnati Conservatory of Music, affiliated with the University of Cincinnati and scheduled to begin its ninth season of concerts in October over the Columbia Broadcasting System, was forced off the air because the school musicians were not union members. In Rochester, New York, the orchestra of the Eastman School of Music was obliged to cancel its radio concerts because many of the participants were not members of the AFM. The Juilliard School of Music in New York was more fortunate. Its concerts were all broadcast over station WNYC, the independent noncommercial municipal outlet, and were not affected by the ban on school orchestras.

The musicians union and its president were criticized by music schools throughout the country. The press, as usual, found many uncomplimentary things to say. It was suggested generally that Petrillo was acting strictly within his contractual and legal rights, but that the labor laws required modification to prevent such display of arbitrary power. Nevertheless the issue concerning school broadcasts quieted down and no notice was taken of it by the press during the entire year of 1943.

The whole affair was precipitated into the open again by the action of Petrillo himself early in 1944. While reviewing the activities of the union to the membership, Petrillo reported boastfully with regard to school bands and orchestras: "However, when all the shooting was over and we came to the summer of 1943, there was no Interlochen high school student orchestra on the air. Nor was there in the year 1943 any other school band or orchestra on the networks and there never will be without the permission of the American Federation of Musicians."[2] This statement was taken by Maddy and sent to the Senate Committee on Interstate Commerce, where the investigation of the union had lapsed. It renewed the interest of Congress in the matter and resulted in the introduction of a bill by Vandenberg in the middle of the year which prohibited interference with the broadcasting of noncommercial cultural or educational programs. The bill passed the Senate in December 1944 but the session of Congress ended before the House of Representatives could take any action in this matter. Vandenberg therefore reintroduced the measure immediately upon the opening of the seventy-ninth Congress in January 1945. The Senate promptly passed the bill again. The proposals included in the bill were quite mild and no specific punitive provisions for violations were attached. The challenge to his power which the Senate vote indicated and the vigorous campaign waged against him by Maddy infuriated Petrillo. The Interlochen camp therefore was put on the unfair list of the AFM. This action made it impractical for any radio network to carry programs from the camp, because union musicians would then be forced to withdraw their services from the network. In addition, it made it impossible for union members to conduct, teach, or play at the camp.

Renewed criticism of Petrillo was expressed and even CIO economist J. Raymond Walsh noted his strong disapproval.[3] The House prepared to toughen the Senate version of the bill. Said Clarence J. Brown, a member of the House of Representatives, in speaking of Petrillo: "This fellow has gone too far. We've got to clip his wings. But we don't want to interfere with the legitimate functions of a union."[4] The committee held hearings over an extended period but Petrillo refused to attend.[5]

The Senate bill was innocuous and would have prevailed but for the increasing attention and criticism which were being directed at Petrillo. Petrillo, however, was under pressure to keep a rapidly growing membership employed. His techniques aroused public resentment. Furthermore, the country was in the middle of a world war and the tactics used by the union were not consistent with governmental manpower measures intended to conserve labor. Congressional scrutiny of the activities of musicians in radio broadcasting therefore was intensified.

Petrillo's efforts to increase the employment of musicians by radio stations may be divided into two parts—one aimed at eliminating the work of nonmembers and the other directed at getting more employment for union musicians. First, he desired to remove all nonunion musicians from the air; and the contracts with the networks provided that only professional musicians could be used on broadcasts. Any exceptions to this rule had to receive the approval of the union. In this way school bands and orchestras were barred. Amateur musicians could play an instrument on the radio only with the permission of the union. Many times such permission was refused, and at other times the program could be given only upon the payment of a standby fee. Major Edward Bowes paid the union an average weekly standby fee of $150. Other programs preferred not to use amateur instrumentalists rather than to pay the standby fees. The union however did not encourage the use of amateurs even when fees were paid and frequently radio stations made no requests for authorization to use amateurs since they anticipated union refusals.

Restrictions also were placed on the use of army bands by the networks. Army bands came under the classification of amateurs and in several cases the union had refused to allow the radio station to put them on. But in 1940 the defense program of the United States was gaining momentum and the army deemed it essential to highlight various radio programs with army bands. The recruiting drive that year included a series of broadcasts depicting army life. When it appeared that the number of requests to play army bands would increase greatly, Petrillo in December 1940 suddenly ordered the networks to eliminate military bands from all programs. He explained the attitude of the union. "This is a good cause and we're all for it, but if we allowed radio stations to put music on the air from Army camps whenever they wanted to they could soon dispense with our men," he said. "We are in favor of their going on the air with programs telling about life in the Army, but we want protection against the loss of jobs for professional musicians. This is going to be a long-range affair. It may last a couple of years, and the sensible thing is to talk it over and make a deal."[6] The "deal" was soon made. The networks guaranteed the union that the use of army music would not result in any curtailment in the employment of studio musicians.

The union has contended for many years that when a nonprofessional musician performs on the radio, the time remaining for professional musicians thereby is contracted. The union has not felt that nonmusical programs would be substituted for the performances of the amateurs. Considering that the major portion of radio time is devoted to music, the union argument may be correct. But the union has failed to give enough weight to two facts—first that records might be used to fill the time and secondly that radio stations have not always used the studio musicians for the full number of hours for which they have been hired under terms of the radio contracts. Additional hours of performance by studio musicians therefore would not necessarily increase the amount of wages paid to the instrumentalists.

The second part of Petrillo's program to increase the employment opportunities of union musicians was positive. He continually exerted pressure on the radio stations to augment the number of musicians that they were employing. This plan abandoned the objective of the 1937 and the 1938 contracts under which the radio stations were required to expend a minimum sum of money for the employment of musicians. Instead it called for the hiring of a specific minimum number of men under guaranteed conditions of employment.

The union assigned each radio station a quota, based on financial status and to some extent on the previous employment record of the station. The greatest economic pressure by the union to achieve its goal could be exerted on affiliated network outlets all over the country for in such cases the network generally quietly intervened; because it was anxious to see the dispute ended. The independent stations, being less dependent on live musicians and more on recorded music could not be subjected by the union to the same degree of pressure.

Some network stations did not want to employ any musicians at all. Others claimed that they did not need the number of men which the union had asked them to take. But these objections were unavailing. The union pointed out that affiliated stations were able to receive from the network and present to the public programs which included the performance of live musicians. These stations, however, were not paying the musicians for this music and therefore should be required to employ a specified number of staff musicians.

The first of these assigned quota cases came during the month of Petrillo's election to the presidency, in June 1940. The union was successful in that and in every other similar case with network stations occurring in the succeeding years in which it made serious efforts to enforce quotas. The union was able to apply three degrees of pressure after making its demands upon the affiliate. First, it could bar name bands from playing for the network. The union was forced to prohibit the network from piping in the name band from the hotel or club at which it was playing in order to get at the individual station because the chains maintained that they were under contract to provide member stations with all programs. Though the network sometimes approved the position taken by its affiliated station, it nevertheless encouraged the station to reach an agreement.

The union's second type of pressure was to pull out the network studio musicians and thereby bring an end to all sustaining musical programs. Even then the network generally was reluctant to cut off its programs from an affiliated station. Though it pointed out to the union that it could not exercise control over the decisions of the stations in the chain, yet the union maintained that the recommendations of the network carried much weight. The third and final step was to call a strike. Networks have sought to avoid strikes because the financial losses involved are substantial. The alternatives open to the chain when a strike is threatened by the musicians are to grant the demands or to suffer the losses involved in the elimination of all commercially sponsored programs having music. Though commercial broadcasts rarely have been cut off, in 1945 the Columbia Broadcasting System had to cancel the Prudential Hour when Petrillo barred Al Goodman and his orchestra from the program. In the same year the National Broadcasting Company's Fitch Bandwagon program lost the services of Artie Shaw and his band when the union had difficulties with one of the system's outlets.

The most spectacular disagreement involved KSTP in St. Paul, Minnesota, an affiliate of NBC. Disputes between the union and the station in 1940 and 1942 over the number of musicians to be employed had been settled with some difficulty. In 1944, the union made new demands which were rejected by the management of the station. A strike of musicians ensued at this station in spite of the pledge which labor had given not to strike during the war period. Mediators were unsuccessful in bringing about any agreement. The decisions and orders of the National War Labor Board directing the end of the strike had no effect on the musicians union. Even the criticisms expressed by William Green, which was an astounding display of initiative, did not influence the AFM.[7] A Minneapolis court ordered the arrest of Petrillo, but the leader of the musicians stayed out of that jurisdiction. At the end of a period of 11 months, KSTP capitulated and signed a contract meeting the terms imposed by the union. The union gained a number of jobs, but it also won the bitter resentment of many members of Congress.

● *The Lea Act*

The House committee closely scrutinized the criticisms leveled against the AFM, for union demands on the radio industry came at a time when manpower shortages were felt acutely in various sectors of the economy. Charges of featherbedding, of excessive employment, and of standby requirements were brought to the attention of the committee. Broadcasters maintained that the standby fee tended to prevent small radio stations from using and developing local amateur talent.

Congressman Clarence F. Lea was soon ready with proposed legislation to curb the power and activities of Petrillo. The proposals were much more severe than anything recommended by the Senate. After a spirited debate in which Petrillo was attacked for being a "Caesar" and in which House members applauded, stamped their feet, and shouted approval, the bill was passed overwhelmingly. A few members of Congress came to the defense of the musicians. Representative Vito Marcantonio of New York expressed fear that the measure might be construed to outlaw strikes. Congressman Benjamin J. Rabin of New York said: ". . . I do not come here to praise Caesar; on the other hand, I do not come here to bury the hard-won rights of labor, . . ."[8] The Senate was induced to accept the House version and President Harry S. Truman signed the measure, known as the Lea Act or Anti-Petrillo Act, in April 1946.[9]

Actually the new law amended some of the provisions of the Communications Act of 1934 which applied to radio broadcasting. The Lea Act made it unlawful to threaten or to compel a broadcaster to: 1. employ more persons than it needed; 2. pay money instead of hiring more persons than it needed; 3. pay more than once for services; 4. pay for services not performed; 5. refrain from broadcasting noncommercial educational programs; 6. refrain from broadcasting radio communications originating outside the United States. With regard to recordings, the law prohibited: 1. payment of exactions for producing or using recordings or transcriptions; 2. imposition of restrictions on production, sales, or use of records or transcriptions; 3. payment of exactions for rebroadcast of programs. Any violations were subject to imprisonment up to one year, or to a fine of not more than $1,000, or to both.

The provisions with regard to recordings were inserted in the bill to prevent several practices which appeared obnoxious to Congress. The AFM had forced a network to cancel the rebroadcast to the Pacific coast, by means of transcriptions, of the Jack Benny and Rudy Vallee programs. The union demanded that the second show should be performed over again by the live actors, or as an alternative that the musicians should receive double pay. The union also had imposed restrictions on the production of records at amateur festivals. The union royalty fund, however, apparently was not affected by this legislation.

Bing Crosby, Bob Hope, Frank Sinatra, and other radio stars opposed the Lea Act because of the severity of its provisions. The American Federation of Radio Artists also seemed to be covered by the law since they engaged in many of the proscribed practices, and some persons believed that writers would be prevented from bargaining for secondary rights to their scripts. The main target, however, had been Petrillo. Petrillo defied the law, declaring that it was unconstitutional.

The coverage of the law was sufficiently broad to permit Petrillo any one of a variety of constitutional tests. The test case was undertaken at radio station WAAF in Chicago. The station had been employing three members of the musicians union, when the AFM requested it to hire three more musicians. When WAAF proclaimed that it did not need any additional musicians, the three union members were called out on strike by Petrillo and a picket was placed before the business premises of the station. Petrillo told reporters gathered in his office: "I'm ready to face the music, gentlemen." Pounding his desk, he continued: "I demand that the Government keep hands off. It should permit the unions and big business to handle their own affairs. . . . We had enough governmental regulation during the war and if anyone thinks labor is going to stand aside and lose all the privileges it has gained during the last thirty years, he is wrong. All labor will be cemented together as never before. We've got to be to save our own hides."[10] At one point he interrupted his discourse and smiled at the reporters. "How am

I doin,' boys?" he asked. Later he obliged photographers by assuming a fighting stance with his left hand thrust out.

The next week Petrillo was told that Representative George A. Dondero of Michigan, who had sponsored the equivalent of the Vandenberg proposal in the House, was considering the introduction of more rigorous curbs on the musicians union. Exploded Petrillo: "Oh, that bum! He represents about 500 people up there in Michigan. He hasn't got the mentality to know what to do. He's a gimme-gimme politician." Then adding a point of view, he said: "Under what law can they make us go to work? The more labor laws they pass, the more labor trouble they're going to have."[11]

When the Federal Bureau of Investigation had completed its report on Petrillo's action at station WAAF, the Department of Justice decided to prosecute. The original prosecuting assistant attorney general, J. Albert Woll, severed his connection with the case when it was disclosed that he was the son of Matthew Woll, one of the AFL vice presidents. During the preliminary hearing Petrillo posted a $1,000 bond by stepping into the district court clerk's office and peeling off ten crisp $100 bills from a roll.

Labor rallied to the support of the musicians union and the AFL convention in 1946 voted to fight the Lea Act. The Civil Liberties Union, which also opposed the law, was prevented from submitting a brief on behalf of Petrillo by United States District Court Judge Walter J. La Buy. The government argued that the AFM was a racketeering organization that had extorted millions of dollars from the radio industry. It told the court that in the months subsequent to the calling of the strike, the work of the three musicians who had walked out was performed by the switchboard operator and another girl in the station's office. The attorney for the government contended that Petrillo was attempting to coerce the employer into hiring more employees than the station required.

Judge La Buy, however, accepted the arguments of the union and in December 1946 he held that the measure was unconstitutional. The court said that the Lea Act conflicted with the first, fifth, and thirteenth amendments to the Constitution of the United States. The first amendment which guaranteed freedom of speech was violated because the law prevented peaceful picketing, a form of speech. The fifth amendment was transgressed because the Act discriminated against radio broadcasting employees and hence did not grant to all persons the equal protection of the laws. The Act also violated the thirteenth amendment prohibiting slavery and involuntary servitude because it regarded as coercion the refusal of some employees to work unless additional employees were engaged.

Under a special rule the government appealed the case directly to the United States Supreme Court. The highest tribunal in a five to three decision overruled the district court in June 1947 and held that the law is constitutional. It said that though the government might have to modify and clarify its complaint against Petrillo, the statute appeared to be a valid one.

Petrillo, whose statement after his victory in the district court was: "Thank God for the Federal Court.",[12] showed his respect for the law when immediately after the adverse verdict in the Supreme Court he said: "This is my country and the Supreme Court makes the final rulings on its laws. No one will ever say that Jim Petrillo fought his country or the Supreme Court. I thought that I had the law on my side, and I made the best fight I knew how. The Supreme Court has spoken, and I bow to its dictates."[13] The fight on this law was by no means over, however, because the case had been remanded to the District Court.[14] Early in 1948, Judge La Buy acquitted Petrillo. He ruled that the government did not prove that Petrillo had attempted to compel WAAF to hire three allegedly unnecessary musicians. Nor did the judge find that the broadcaster had been coerced.[15] More definite court interpretations of the Lea Act must await new test cases.

Meanwhile the National Music Camp remained in the news. When it reopened its doors in July 1945, Maddy, in defiance of Petrillo, was there to conduct the orchestra. He was ordered to appear before the international executive board to explain why he disregarded the action of the union under which the camp had been placed on the unfair list. After a trial in which Petrillo deliberately did not participate officially, Maddy was expelled from the union early in 1946. It is possible that this penalty could have been invoked against him long before that time, for engaging in conduct prejudicial to the welfare of the union. The national officers, however, had not chosen to use his statements to the press and his written reports to the public as grounds for their action. Their case against Maddy was much stronger because they had waited.

Even after the passage of the Lea Act no network was willing to sponsor an Interlochen program. The camp had been broadcasting a musical program for four hours every week over the Michigan State College station at Lansing, Michigan, an independent station having no link with the AFM. New Congressional hearings dealing with the AFM were held in 1947 by a subcommittee, under the chairmanship of Representative Carroll D. Kearns, of the Committee on Education and Labor. Petrillo threatened to expel Kearns, a music teacher, from the AFM when the Congressman indicated that he might partake as guest conductor in a music festival at Interlochen.[16] Kearns had given varying statements to the press, but in the end he stayed away from the camp.

As a result of Congressional hearings and further discussions in the summer of 1947, the union reversed its policies in several respects. It permitted school and military bands to make recordings. The records, however, could be cut only for the exclusive use of the schools and colleges and for educational purposes. In September 1947, the AFM signed a code of ethics with representatives for the Music Educators National Conference and the American Association of School Administrators regarding the areas within which each was to operate.[17] This agreement convinced Petrillo that there would be no competition between school bands and professional musicians for employment, so he ended the ban on radio broadcasting by school children. After a period of five years in which they had been barred from the networks, schools once more were permitted to resume broadcasting. But the National Music Camp at Interlochen, Michigan, has remained on the unfair list of the American Federation of Musicians. Despite the Lea Act, therefore, radio networks have refrained from broadcasting any Interlochen concerts.

The Lea Act represented the first significant legislative curb imposed on the activities of labor unions subsequent to the introduction of the New Deal labor policy by the federal government. The enactment of legislation such as the Lea Act, curtailing the activities and power of trade unions was inevitable, however, given the temper of Congress in 1946. The practices of featherbedding, of standbys, and of banning various groups from radio broadcasting had irked many people who were not fully conversant with the issues.

It should be recognized that policies similar to those adopted by the musicians union, directed towards increased employment, were approved and enforced by many other labor organizations. Make-work problems are certainly more serious on the railroads and in the building trades. But the methods used by the musicians union constantly were arousing bitterness and resentment. Attention had been centered on Petrillo and every move he made was deemed worthy of newspaper headlines. The public relations of the union were rather unsatisfactory. Weber had enjoyed as much power as Petrillo and had been able to win substantial gains for the musicians during his period of leadership, yet he had kept the AFM in the background and had avoided much of the unfavorable criticism hurled against the union during the presidency of Petrillo. It is true that Petrillo has gained his objectives more quickly, but only at a heavier cost to the union.

The Interlochen dispute was an unfortunate episode; especially since it probably would have been settled satisfactorily if Maddy had taken up the matter with Petrillo directly instead of seeking assistance from Congress and the press. Banning school children from taking part in musical radio programs has not appeared to be a satisfactory technique for alleviating the unemployment of musicians in any appreciable manner. The number of such amateur programs has been extremely small. But the hostile sentiments engendered by this dispute were magnified by certain union practices which had existed for a long time. At the culmination of public disapproval, the Lea Act was passed.

"Now Congressmen, make a law to make us go to work,
chew on that one for a while."

JAMES CAESAR PETRILLO

• Another Record Ban

The year 1948 was one in which major decisions were made
by the American Federation of Musicians. At the beginning of
January disputes were raging with regard to the manufacture
of records, the negotiation of radio contracts, the future of frequency modulation, and the performance of live music over
television. Each of these difficulties essentially was adjusted by
the end of that year. Congress had expected the Lea Act to
solve the labor problems of the broadcasters. The only significant immediate effect, however, was that the union abandoned
its practice of collecting standby fees from the radio industry.
Over a longer period, the number of staff musicians employed
by radio stations declined substantially.

Although a possibility exists that some sections in the Lea
Act affect the establishment of a recording and transcription
fund, no test of these provisions ever has been made. When
Congress passed the Labor Management Relations Act (Taft-
Hartley Act) [1] in 1947, union welfare funds clearly became
subject to federal regulation. The law gave detailed specifi-
cations regarding the provisions necessary in an agreement
between labor and management which creates such a fund.
The purpose of the welfare fund must be set down in writ-
ing. Equal control over expenditures of the money in the
fund must be exercised by representatives of the union and of
the employers. If these representatives do not agree upon a
matter within their jurisdiction, they must select an impartial
umpire to make the final decision. The law states that the fund
may be used solely and exclusively for the benefit of the em-

ployees, including their families and dependents, of those employers making the contribution.

The American Federation of Musicians had stated the general purpose for which the money in its royalty fund would be used. Minute details, however, had not been given in the agreements. But the recording contracts expired at the end of 1947 and any extension would be subject to the provisions of the Taft-Hartley law. Petrillo refused to modify the basic conditions with regard to the recording fund which he had included in the recording contracts of 1943. He was at first reluctant to allow the agents of the recording companies to have any voice in determining the disposition of the money in the fund. He also felt that the fund would lose its main value to the AFM if it could be used only for the benefit of those musicians who made the records. The latter objection was removed, however, by the United States Supreme Court decision that in defining the term "employee" technical and traditional concepts were not the sole guides to be used, but that account could be taken of the more relevant economic and statutory considerations.[2] Although all musicians thus could benefit from a welfare fund, the Lea Act and the Taft-Hartley Act made it difficult for the union to exercise that degree of control which it desired. (As finally set up, the recorders agreed to pay royalties into a fund to be used for the benefit of the public, so that the law's provisions regarding the employees who might benefit from a welfare fund apparently do not apply.)

Petrillo had warned the nation that the AFM would resist any attempt to prevent the union from collecting royalties on records. He had announced that if the circumstances warranted, he would "send out a simple little letter. We'll just say, 'Gentlemen on such and such a date, members of the American Federation of Musicians will not be permitted to perform in the making of recordings and transcriptions.'" Petrillo continued: "Now Congressmen, make a law to make us go to work, chew on that one for a while."[3]

Congress passed the Labor Management Relations Act and Petrillo subsequently sent the letter he had promised. From the convention of 1947, Petrillo had received the authority to order the members of the union to cease making recordings upon the expiration of the contract. He also was given permission either to negotiate new agreements with the recording companies or to go into the recording business in competition with them. At the end of October 1947, however, he notified the recording and transcription companies that contracts with them would not be renewed. He emphasized that the union irrevocably had committed itself to a policy of never again working for any recording company.

Petrillo's avowal that the record ban was permanent was not given too much weight by the industry or by the public because he had made similar statements on the previous occasions when he had banned recordings. It seemed clear that Petrillo was attempting to gain a stronger bargaining position. The record companies were not too concerned with the union's threat to go into the business because it was apparent that such action would violate the antitrust laws. If the union were the sole recorder of instrumentalists, competition would be eliminated and trade would be restrained. The union itself recognized these implications and refrained from moving in that direction.

On January 1, 1948, the production of musical records ceased in the United States and Canada. But the major recording companies already had had experience with a ban and were prepared. Since they had been given sufficient warning in advance by Petrillo, they had cut enormous stockpiles of master records. The backlog was so great that a supply of new musical records would, if necessary, have been available to the companies for several years. Only the newly composed popular song hits could not be recorded. The large recording companies had accumulated so much material that they would have sustained losses if an immediate lifting of the record ban had occurred. The smaller and financially weaker record companies, however, were not prepared for a long contest with the union.

The AFM had the support of its entire membership, of many labor unions in the United States, and of the unions of musicians of Great Britain, Mexico, Cuba, Chile, and South Africa. Petrillo emphasized that the record ban had been reimposed because of the technological unemployment resulting from the use of records. He referred particularly to the greater number of juke boxes in use, to the increase in the number of disk jockeys, and to the growth in wired music service.

There were several reasons, however, which induced Petrillo

to negotiate with the record and transcription companies. First, he had told members of Congress that he would be willing to do so. Secondly, there was public pressure exerted to remove the restrictions on recordings. Thirdly, the number of records produced and sent into the United States from foreign countries expanded throughout the period of the ban and served to weaken the control of the AFM over the situation. Furthermore, the production of bootleg records—in which musicians work anonymously or under fictitious names—increased.[4] Although stations employing live musicians could not use such records, those radio broadcasters who depended entirely on recorded music were under no such handicap. Fourthly, there was some talk in the industry of signing musicians to long-term recording contracts so that they would not be reluctant to risk expulsion from the union for recording. Recording companies could not expect to secure the services of leading orchestras and name bands, however, because violation of the ban by any musician would result in his expulsion from the union. Expelled musicians would be barred from playing in unionized establishments, and it has been in those places where professional musicians normally have earned the major source of their income. Fifthly, charges had been filed by the transcription companies with the NLRB against the AFM, the New York local, and the Los Angeles local in May 1948 claiming that the union had violated the Taft-Hartley law because the record ban had compelled the transcription companies to cease doing business with the radio stations. This represented, they said, a secondary boycott. Subsequently, however, in December 1948, the regional director of the NLRB in New York ruled that the record ban did not violate the Taft-Hartley law and he refused to issue any complaints in this matter.[5] Sixthly, the threat of Congressional action to break the efficacy of the ban was a distinct possibility.

In February 1948, Petrillo had eased the record ban to permit the networks to record some of their shows when the disk was to be used only once and then discarded. It was not until September that he was willing to negotiate regarding a general solution to the problem. In December agreements were reached with the record and transcription companies under which a music performance trust fund was set up to provide employment for instrumental musicians, whether or not members of the union, and to promote the appreciation of instrumental music by the general public. No admission fees might be charged. The record companies were to pay a percentage of the retail price of each record sold, ranging from one per cent of the price of records under a dollar to two and a half per cent of the price of records over two dollars, into the fund. The transcription companies were to pay three per cent of the gross revenues derived from leasing transcriptions. When the Solicitor of Labor of the Department of Labor and the Attorney General of the United States found that the trustee would not be appointed by or be a representative of the AFM, they held that the trust agreement did not violate the Taft-Hartley law. The contracts between the union and the major companies were signed on December 14, 1948 and recording work was resumed immediately. The first trustee, Samuel R. Rosenbaum, was appointed by the companies. He was favorably regarded by the union. Successor trustees are to be selected by the Secretary of Labor. Wage scales remained the same as under the October 1946 agreement.[6]

Since the agreement extends through the end of 1953, a relatively long period of stability has been assured. In May 1949, Rosenbaum outlined the procedures under which the music performance trust fund would be administered. In general, the trustee was satisfied with the operation of the recording and transcription fund, and therefore modeled the new fund along those lines. Allocations to the locals now are made twice a year.[7]

Radio stations and networks were vitally interested in the outcome of the record controversy because of the financial link between the two industries and because radio programs have depended on the use of records for much of the music they present. There was fear that a strike by network musicians would materialize at the expiration of the contract in January 1948. Networks had been set to meet a strike by preparing in advance many transcriptions of commercial advertisements which use music. This material would have lasted several months. The union and the networks, however, came to a basic understanding and agreed to extend the expiring agreement temporarily. The union announced two major concessions. It would no longer apply pressure on the networks to force affiliated stations to hire additional musicians. The AFM, which gave no indication of any alternative tactics, had threatened to play only on local programs, and thus cut off affiliated stations. The AFM also agreed to modify its policy on frequency modulation (FM) broadcasts.

● *Developments in Frequency Modulation*

FM was invented and perfected by Major Edwin H. Armstrong in the 1930's. It is a system of radio broadcasting which provides the listener with high fidelity reproduction of sound and with staticless reception. The first high-power FM station began to operate in 1939. Since then FM stations have increased in number very rapidly and it is possible that they may eventually replace many amplitude modulation (AM) or standard broadcasting stations. Programs prepared for AM may be sent over FM channels with only a slight increase in engineering costs.

The standard broadcasters immediately recognized the potential importance of FM and they secured FM outlets. Many other persons and business organizations, however, who had no connection with AM stations also built FM stations. The development of the invention of frequency modulation has shown slow progress because the public has not had the disposition to buy receiving sets of this type. On the other hand, there have not been many entrepreneurs willing to risk capital in order to develop the invention during the period of its infancy. Radio networks had the most money to spend on FM, but they did not want to invest more than the minimum necessary to gain a strong foothold.

The original intention of the Federal Communications Commission, which regulates the radio industry, was to require separate programs to be broadcast on AM and FM. This policy presumably was intended to give all groups interested in developing the new field an equal start. When the networks protested that the additional expense would impose a financial burden that would retard the rapid development of frequency modulation, the FCC reversed its position. It ruled that the same program could be broadcast on both mediums simultaneously. As a result, by 1944, an accelerated development of FM was forecast. Though the New York local of the AFM had protested the practice of simultaneous broadcasting over AM and

FM in 1942 and 1943, the networks continued to engage in it. In September 1944, immediately after the New York City station of NBC received a commercial license for its FM transmitter, Petrillo notified the four major networks that use of musicians on FM programs without permission from the AFM was a violation of the radio contracts. Some correspondence between the networks and the union was interchanged, but no solution was reached. The networks maintained that they had to transmit programs over FM without any additional charges to the advertisers because simultaneous broadcasts did not increase the number of people able to hear the programs. Rates to advertisers have been based upon the potential number of listeners and not the actual size of the audience.

The musicians union claimed that the act of duplicating programs over AM and FM without increasing the advertising rates put independent FM stations at a competitive disadvantage. Advertisers would not be encouraged to put programs on FM stations only, if they could have them aired over both mediums. This advertising policy would hurt the struggling FM outlets. The AFM, however, wanted to protect the growing FM industry because it had envisioned much future employment for its members in it. Some of the independent FM broadcasters also opposed the simultaneous transmission of programs.

Petrillo and the networks were unable to break the impasse, but Petrillo had the final word. After wrangling for a year, during which time the networks continued to send AM programs over FM outlets, Petrillo ordered that beginning on October 29, 1945, double crews of musicians would have to be employed on all duplicated programs. Networks were not permitted to feed chain programs played by orchestras on AM stations to FM affiliates. Moreover, this ruling was applicable to local independent AM stations. Locals of the AFM, however, were permitted to make separate contracts to supply the services of musicians who were to be used for broadcasting exclusively on independent FM stations. The networks complied with these orders because the radio contracts were silent on the FM question and because of the implied threat of a strike by the musicians. They did not employ additional musicians but they stopped duplicating programs with music.

The policy of the musicians union was attacked by the radio

industry. Public clamor also was directed against the union's position. The Federal Communications Commission was powerless to step into this labor dispute although the broadcasters and the public requested it to do so several times. When Paul A. Porter, Chairman of the FCC, addressed an interested audience, he said jocularly: "The FCC is in favor of duplicate programs but it appears that Petrillo has overruled the FCC." A woman in the audience asked "where Petrillo got all his power." Porter replied: "My dear lady that question has me puzzled. All I can say is that he didn't get it from the FCC."[8]

After the networks rejected Petrillo's plan, they decided to shut down all FM transmitters. They took advantage of the occasion and installed different transmitting equipment. This operation was necessary because the FCC had assigned new wave lengths for FM. The shift could best be executed by going off the air for several months.

Those persons who had predicted that Petrillo would quickly modify his order were wrong. For two and a half years the AFM did not set any wage scales for FM network broadcasts and no musical programs were duplicated, though some independent FM stations continued to broadcast live music. Furthermore, in September 1947 the AFM prohibited FM networks from using musicians. Pleas by both AM and FM networks to the union to alter its policy were unavailing even after passage of the Lea Act. At the end of January 1948, however, while negotiations were in progress to draw up new radio contracts with the networks, Petrillo rescinded his order affecting FM. The duplication of programs over AM and FM was permitted; and FM networks could employ musicians. This action, however, put stations operating on FM only at a competitive disadvantage in securing commercial sponsors.

The decision of the union to permit duplication of programs without asking for additional compensation for musicians was welcomed by the radio industry and by the public. Except for the fact that the established standard broadcasting companies had a tremendous advantage over other FM operators, the development of FM could be pushed forward rapidly. Yet the AM networks, which were in the strongest financial and technical position to advance FM, were not especially anxious to do so because of their tremendous investment in standard broadcasting and because of the uncertainties regarding the future of the radio industry brought about by the growth of television (TV). The expansion of frequency modulation broadcasting therefore has been very slow.

Simultaneously with the long negotiations regarding FM, the union was engaged in working out a policy in connection with the other major technological invention affecting musicians. The type of agreements subsequently reached for television were entirely different.

● *The Television Controversy*

The idea of television is old, but public broadcasting service on this medium did not begin in the United States until 1939. Commercial programs began to be telecast in 1941. Much of the broadcast time, however, was devoted to experimentation and to the development of new techniques and procedures. In television too, radio networks assumed the lead. Monetary outlays during the developmental period were high though it was uncertain whether the future returns would show the expenditures to have been wisely made.

At first the AFM cooperated with the industry. During 1943, Petrillo set the television scale for musicians at $18 an hour, and put a lower price on rehearsals. In February 1945, however, the international executive board prohibited musicians from playing on any form of television program. This action immediately affected two of the three major forms of video presentation—television programs are divided among studio broadcasts, mobile unit pickups, and films. Musicians were cut off from the first two of these types of broadcasts. The televising of motion pictures containing music was prohibited subsequently, as already described, by contract with the film producers in 1946. The 1945 ban was not coupled with any demand, suggestion, or request. It applied even to those performances where the music merely would be heard and the musician would not be included in the field of vision. However, rumors that the object of the ban was to help the film industry take control of television from the radio industry were denied by spokesmen for the film producers.

The development of TV was hampered by the action of the musicians union, but the industry continued to grow. Aside from the musicians themselves, it was mainly the public which suffered because it was barred from enjoying many possible types of television entertainment. Television broadcasters had greater difficulty in meeting the minimum program time requirements of the FCC with suitable presentations. The attitude of the union, however, was understandable. It was based on the fear that the disastrous unemployment which had occurred in the theaters after the introduction of sound films would be repeated with the development of television. Since television programs may be produced by filming the show first and presenting it at a later time over the video channel, Petrillo feared that eventually canned television or the kinescope would displace the live musicians employed during the early stages of development. That is, for example, a television program of a famous name band playing musical selections would be filmed and used over again many times subsequently. The union was trying to prevent the creation of a television record industry which would become as important to television as phonograph records have been to radio. Petrillo argued that before committing the AFM to any television policy, he wanted to have a clearer idea of the direction in which video programs were heading. The union also desired some assurance that the approximately $23,000,000 in income which its members have been receiving from radio would not be lost by an inaccurate decision regarding the future of television.

The solution had to be based on the assurance to musicians that excessive use would not be made of kinescopes. The hesitancy of the AFM to commit itself had justification. A decision on its part probably would set the pattern for the future contractual relations in an industry that seemed destined to replace radio. The musicians union, therefore, either would have to impose an outright prohibition on canned television programs by the broadcasters or, as an alternative, it would have to demand a royalty fund into which payments would be made each time a canned musical program was televised. The union was not concerned particularly with live television broadcasts, since no displacement problem was presented by them.

In March 1948, Petrillo announced that a new three-year agreement with the radio networks had been signed. Contracts between the New York, Chicago, and Los Angeles locals and the four major networks were renewed without change in either the wage scales or the number of staff musicians to be employed. But the contracts were modified to permit the use of musicians on television at wage rates that would be determined every few months during television's developmental stage. The contracts further were altered to permit the simultaneous use of musicians on AM and FM and to allow broadcasting of cooperative programs.

At the end of April the FM and the networks agreed to put television pay scales into effect for a six-month period, beginning on May 1. The rates set were lower than those established for radio musicians, but depended on whether a network or local program was involved. The agreement permitted musical programs to be filmed for storage in network files or for a single presentation at regular television wage scales. The agreement subsequently was extended until April 1, 1949, at which time a new one year contract was executed with the networks under which the pay scales were increased. Locals retained the power to make scales for local television broadcasts emanating from independently owned stations.

The negotiations at the beginning of 1951 between the radio networks and the AFM locals in New York, Los Angeles, and Chicago over the terms of a new agreement to go into effect on February 1, 1951 were not successful. Early in March the New York local authorized a strike against the networks, subject to the approval of the AFM. The Los Angeles local authorized the AFM to take such action as it might deem necessary. Petrillo, backed by the international executive board, decided to take over the negotiations on March 13. He maintained that such action was in the interest of all musicians.[9] In a relatively short time he reached an agreement on the basic conditions for a three-year contract extending to February 1, 1954. It included radio, television, and television film contracts.

Many of the issues between the American Federation of Musicians and the radio broadcasting and television industries were resolved. The main gains made by the union were a general increase in radio wage rates of 15 per cent and an agreement to set the vacation period at two weeks. The broadcasters successfully rejected demands to reduce the amount of recorded music they would play and to increase the number of staff musicians. Wage rates for television programs were equalized with those prevailing in the radio industry.

The union agreed to permit simulcasting over AM and FM, AM and TV, FM and TV, and AM, FM, and TV. No extra charge is made by musicians for a simulcast over AM and FM, but if the program is played simultaneously over the radio and over television, an additional sum, depending on whether the program is a sustaining or a commercial broadcast, is paid to them.

The musicians were not given any additional staff employment for television broadcasts. They will, however, receive many single engagements on this medium. Some concessions were made by the union in regard to kinescopes or television recording. Such recordings may be shown only once in any city on a station not receiving the original broadcast, but affiliated with the network at the time the film was made. The kinescope must be taken at the time of the regularly scheduled live broadcast and must be shown within 60 days of production. A separate television film agreement was negotiated with the networks under which films could be made and shown providing the networks would pay five per cent of the receipts derived from leasing the films into a music performance trust fund.

Cooperative programs are paid for at the same rates as if sponsored by a single advertiser. Participating broadcasts (one integrated unit, but without a specific time allocation to advertisers), segmented shows (where there is a specific time allocation to sponsors), and composite programs (a combination of the two) may be aired only if musicians are paid at higher wage rates. The contracts also require the networks to obtain permission from the union before sending any musical program abroad.

In 1951, the AFM also concluded its first major contracts with motion picture companies for televising motion picture films. In contracts with the Republic Pictures, a member of the Motion Picture Producers Association, and the Monogram Company the union agreed to permit the use of films on TV provided that the musical score was replayed and that five per cent of the receipts of the companies from the lease of the films would be paid into a music performance trust fund. The preceding year agreements had been reached with several small companies for the production of TV films under similar conditions.[10]

The union thus has reached a stage where relatively stable relations have been achieved with the recording, radio, and television industries. Some major issues still remain. But it appears that there will not be much controversy engaged in by musicians in these industries for at least a few years.

● *Congressional Investigations*

The union's policies in connection with technological progress and mechanical reproduction of music has aroused public interest and criticism. Congressional inquiry into the objectives and practices of the AFM was renewed in 1947, because it appeared that neither the earlier investigations nor the Lea Act in which they had terminated had affected or influenced Petrillo or the union markedly. The victory of the Republican party in the 1946 Congressional elections, gave Fred A. Hartley, Jr. the chairmanship of the House Committee on Education and Labor. In February 1947, just after the eightieth Congress was organized, he introduced a resolution to give his committee the power to subpoena witnesses and to administer oaths. The House of Representatives agreed to this resolution.

The committee had received a number of complaints regarding the practices of the musicians union. Although other organizations were investigated also, Hartley was interested especially in some of the policies and activities of the AFM. Dr. Joseph E. Maddy had complained to the committee about the Interlochen situation. Charges also had been brought to the committee by Earl Carroll that the Los Angeles local of the union had forced him to maintain an orchestra larger than he needed for the operation of his theater-restaurant in that city. The committee subsequently suspected that officers and members of local 47 in Los Angeles had been guilty of intimidating and punishing Earl Carroll for bringing the charges. Hartley ordered a thorough investigation of the charges. He appointed a subcommittee of three members to determine whether any laws had been violated and whether any witnesses had been coerced. Carroll D. Kearns, of Pennsylvania, who was a member of the musicians union, was named chairman. The subcommittee was anxious to hear Petrillo testify and it served him with a subpoena, though it delayed calling upon him until the United States

Supreme Court had ruled that the Lea Act was constitutional. As a result, in order to be at the disposal of the subcommittee Petrillo was forced to cancel a scheduled trip to Europe. He had hoped to formulate a plan, in cooperation with the British musicians, under which a world federation of musicians would be organized. This plan now must await a more propitious occasion.

Most of the testimony was taken in Los Angeles. Much of it was concerned with the policies and activities of the Los Angeles local. Petrillo, however, testified in Washington, D. C., in July. The president of the AFM reiterated many of the arguments he had previously expressed regarding the necessity of protecting the employment opportunities of musicians. Petrillo claimed that musicians who do not work full time in the profession, but who desire to do so, must be considered unemployed. No accurate study of the working activities and schedules of the membership ever has been made. It was estimated in 1947, however, that about 32,400 of the 216,000 members of the AFM earned their livelihood by working exclusively as musicians. About twice that number gained part of their livelihood in other vocations. More than 86,000 musicians had dropped their instruments because there was no work for them or because they developed other interests.[11] Throughout his testimony, Petrillo manifested a disposition to compromise the issues in dispute.

During one exchange with the committee, Petrillo said to Congressman Kearns: "By the way, I understand you are a good musician. *Mr. Kearns.* Thank you, Mr. Petrillo. *Mr. Petrillo.* I mean that. *Mr. Nixon.* Do you understand he is also a good Congressman? *Mr. Petrillo.* Not yet. I will tell you more about that when we get through here."[12] At another time, Petrillo said: "While we are talking about the Government, what are we going to do about President Truman? He plays the piano. *Mr. Kearns.* I will make the suggestion that we pay him as a stand-by. How is that?"[13]

Petrillo made several immediate and tangible concessions as a result of his appearance before the Congressional subcommittee. He executed a code of ethics with the American Association of School Administrators and with the Music Educators National Conference. This document permitted music students to perform in public, broadcast, and make audition records in furtherance of their musical education, if such activity was of a nonprofit, noncommercial, and noncompetitive nature. Petrillo also agreed to permit the service bands of the armed forces to make recordings to be used strictly for educational purposes. Furthermore, Petrillo restored the union licenses to two bookers who had complained to the subcommittee that their licenses had been revoked without good cause.

The subcommittee found that the Los Angeles local had adjusted its dispute with Earl Carroll in a manner satisfactory to all concerned. It therefore recommended that that phase of the investigation should be closed without any further action. The report which it submitted to Congress, however, urged the enactment of legislation which would end the monopolistic practices of trade unions and bar unions from licensing employers who want to do business. The subcommittee said of Petrillo and the AFM: "The continued exercise of such tyrannical power by any individual or group should not be countenanced nor tolerated in a free Republic."[14]

The House Committee on Education and Labor began hearings in January 1948 to consider the legislation proposed by the subcommittee to forbid monopolistic practices of labor unions which are injurious to the public interest. Representatives of industry testified at length that the power of the AFM was excessive and should be curbed. One witness became so irritated, he said: "I have an ulcer which I would like to give to Mr. Petrillo."[15] Spokesmen for the recorders, however, declared that they were in favor of continuing payments under a royalty plan, but that the Labor Management Relations Act had interposed an obstacle to the peaceful settlement of the recording controversy. Petrillo also was called to the witness stand. He declared that he was willing to negotiate all issues, except the ban on records. He agreed, however, to Hartley's suggestion that a secret poll of musicians should be taken to determine whether members of the AFM really favored the ban on recordings; the vote never was held. Petrillo repeated that he had no objections to the manufacture of records that would be used only in the home, if such a system could be worked out. He was opposed to the production of that 20 per cent of the records which is used commercially.

Petrillo was told by one of the members of the committee that President Truman disagreed with him regarding the amount of money available to the public for consumption expenditures. "*Mr. Owens*. . . . And now, do you not believe the President? *Mr. Petrillo*. I won't contradict the President. *Mr. Owens*. Well, it is true; is it not? *Mr. Petrillo*. After all, he is a potential member of the union; he is a piano player. *Mr. Owens*. That is right. He was more than a piano player, Mr. Petrillo. He had several other occupations, as well."[16]

Various caustic and sarcastic remarks were interjected into the testimony. The chairman related that he had been told by a member of the AFM: "You know, in music when we say 'fortissimo,' we speak of loud music; when we say 'pianissimo,' we speak of soft music; and when we say 'Petrillo,' we speak of no music."[17] At one point, a discussion occurred regarding the qualifications necessary for membership in the union. Both the witness and the Congressman who questioned him felt that the admission standards were too low." *Mr. Hoffman*. . . . the fellow who carries a record from one room to another and puts it on the machine—*Mr. Asch*. A platter turner. *Mr. Hoffman*. Is eligible to become a member of the union. *Mr. Asch*. I am not sure. They probably would make him a cymbal player and let him bang the cymbals and take him in. *Mr. Hoffman*. . . . May a janitor, for example, become a member of the union? . . . *The Chairman*. Let us be in order."[18] It is therefore a curious fact that at the beginning of 1950 a report by a committee of the American Conference of Academic Deans assailed the medical profession for using "Petrillo economics" to keep down the number of students admitted to medical schools. Petrillo denied the implied charge, pointing out that admission to his union was relatively easy.[19]

The first major result of these hearings was that Petrillo rescinded the ban on the simulcast or duplication of AM and FM programs. No double crew or additional pay was necessary. This action by Petrillo already has been discussed. No legislation was enacted by Congress as a result of these hearings and no further investigations of the AFM have been made.

The history of Congressional investigations of the AFM has demonstrated one salient characteristic. The union of musicians has corrected many of the undesirable practices and eliminated some of the abuses of which it has been guilty, as a result of public hearings. Airing the problems before a legislative committee has been effective in bringing the pressure of public opinion to bear on the union and has served to narrow the area of many disputes. Vengeful Congressional legislation, however, has not solved the troublesome and vexatious problems faced by the musicians.

"The machine of itself brings certain dangers and certain benefits. To my mind the latter outweigh the former."
STUART CHASE

• The Stature of Petrillo

During the decade in which he has served as president of the American Federation of Musicians, James C. Petrillo has gained tremendous stature as a labor leader. Today, as he passes 60 years of age, he is emerging slowly as one of labor's elder statesmen. He is respected by the overwhelming majority of the members of his union and by the employers with whom he deals. Although, for example, there is much more amiability between Petrillo and the film producers than between Petrillo and the heads of the radio networks, his integrity is recognized by all with whom he negotiates. In January 1951, Petrillo was elected a vice president of the American Federation of Labor, succeeding Joseph N. Weber in that position.

As Petrillo has increased his knowledge of the music industry and as he has perfected the techniques of bargaining with employers, he simultaneously has become milder. His position of control in the union is so complete that he no longer has to undertake vigorous campaigns against employers to demonstrate his value to the organization. Employers frequently are more willing to negotiate with Petrillo, whom they consider more reasonable, than with local officers, whose more extensive demands would be more costly if granted. There have already been several minor indications that some local leaders are anxiously waiting for the time when Petrillo will be ready to retire. At present, though faint rumblings may be heard in a number of locals, no member of the AFM poses a threat to Petrillo's dominance.

It is a common practice for Petrillo to take action on certain matters first and then secure the concurrence of the international executive board. Sometimes, however, it is not practicable to wait for approval before taking the action. During his service as president, Petrillo has built up a good record. He was responsible for the unionization of all the nonunion professional musicians who had not yet joined the AFM. Several jurisdictional disputes were brought to an amicable termination. Written contracts were negotiated with the record companies and film producers for the first time. The principle of a royalty payment into a fund used for the benefit of the musicians union was formulated first in connection with the recording and transcription companies and then carried over to the film and television industries. Favorable agreements were concluded with the radio and television networks. The most serious setback suffered by the AFM in the last 10 years was the passage of the Lea Act, the main result of which was that the network affiliated radio stations and the independent stations were able to reduce or eliminate the services rendered to them by live musicians.

Weber had had a relatively favorable press. From the time Petrillo assumed the presidency of the international union in 1940, however, the new head of the AFM served as the butt of vitriolic attacks by the newspapers and was caricatured unfavorably by the cartoonists. Since 1948, when Petrillo decided to hire a public relations adviser and to spend many tens of thousands of dollars in influencing public opinion, there has been an evident change in the treatment he has received from reporters. In most descriptions of him which now appear, he is considered to be a human being.

There have been several matters in which Petrillo has shown an especial interest recently. He has clearly recognized and told the members of the union that when business conditions deteriorate, it is necessary for the AFM to make concessions to employers who are hard pressed to stay in business.[1] It is mainly for this reason that the AFM has been waging a vigorous campaign during the last few years to have the 20 per cent amusement tax imposed on the prices charged by establishments where live musicians are employed repealed. The union has maintained that the decline in employment of musicians in restaurants, night clubs, hotels, dance halls, and theaters might be arrested if the tax were eliminated. The tax has encouraged some employers to substitute wired music or juke boxes for the live musicians. The employer thus is able to derive a revenue and to eliminate the 20 per cent tax from his establishment.

The AFM has become more concerned with political activity. Petrillo always has supported the Democratic party, but the position of the union now is more clearly formulated and regularly described in the pages of the *International Musician*. The attitude generally follows the one taken by Labor's League for Political Education of the AFL, to which body the musicians union has given considerable financial support. The American Federation of Musicians has made significant contributions in assisting the government to conduct the "cold" war. The AFM sometimes has donated its services and on other occasions has waived its rules to make music available for the Voice of America programs and to assist the Economic Cooperation Administration.[2]

• *Technological Issues*

The activities of the American Federation of Musicians affect a quarter of a million members directly, but also have an impact on the life of the nation. Leisure time and relaxation for millions in the population are linked intimately with musical entertainment. The decisions of the musicians union therefore should be scrutinized closely by the public. Of most immediate concern to the country has been the policy of the union in connection with technological change. The position of the union on this matter has been formulated slowly.

The musicians union suffered severe unemployment when the sound films were introduced into the theaters. Since that time the union has sought to arrest the development and utilization of many mechanical devices and technological advances in the field of music. Gradually, a distinction between the different inventions has been made. Frequency modulation has been recognized as a medium which will not involve any displacement of musicians in the future. The television industry, except for the use of kinescopes, seems to be of similar character. The union decided therefore, though reluctantly, not to require double crews when simultaneous broadcasts are made, although musicians do receive a higher wage rate for simulcasts involving TV. The AFM also abandoned its attempt to impose especially onerous conditions on cooperatively sponsored programs.

The situation differs when the musician helps to produce a commodity which may be used subsequently to eliminate his services. The first important invention of this kind was the phonograph record. The problem has divided itself into two parts. First, although the musician has been paid a high wage scale by the company when he has performed for the recording, he has had no further claim to remuneration no matter how much income the company has earned from the record. Secondly, the unlimited use of records by the radio stations has reduced the need for live talent. In the last few years the disk jockey and the juke box have become national institutions.

The AFM seems to have solved the first aspect of the problem. The union has not been concerned primarily with the recording musicians because the income of this group has been high. Instead, the union has endeavored to assist those musicians who supposedly are unemployed because of the encroachment of records. Although the music performance trust fund has been adopted as the means to that end, several alternatives had been possible.

It has been proposed that the recording companies should lease or rent their product, in a manner similar to the transcription companies, rather than sell it outright. This procedure would have enabled the companies to maintain control over the phonographic record and prevent its unauthorized use by radio stations, in juke boxes, and for other public commercial services. The use of the records in the home, of course, would not be supervised. This plan would have made it feasible for a fee to be paid by radio stations and juke boxes for the use of records. Court decisions which have nullified stipulations limiting the use of the records to the home would have become inapplicable, because records no longer would be sold.

It also has been proposed that the copyright law should be modified. British laws provide for the payment of a fee to musicians each time their records are used. The United States copyright law of 1909 provides that the composer and librettist of a musical composition should receive royalties from radio stations playing their records and from publishers of their songs.[3] Under a contract with the recording company, the band leader gets a royalty on sales. Musicians in the band, however, are *guaranteed* to receive nothing beyond the union scale, though they *may* be paid above the scale.

The AFM admitted that performing musicians have been well paid. It felt therefore that the copyright income should be utilized for the benefit of unemployed musicians. This condition would have necessitated transferring the receipts of the copyright from the performer to the union or assigning the copyright to the manufacturer under a contract that a specified proportion of the receipts would be turned over to the union. Neither the union nor the recording companies were enthusiastic to obtain copyright legislation of this nature. The union would have been burdened with tax and administrative difficulties and possibly with the resentment of recording musicians who would receive none of the royalties. The companies were not disposed to accept the principle of turning over copyright moneys to be used for the benefit of musicians whom they never had employed. Although copyright legislation might have been able to produce the income which the union sought, the AFM never zealously strove to obtain such provisions.

The manufacture of transcriptions never raised serious complications because the industry is small and the product is leased, not sold, to radio stations. The union receives a percentage of the income of the transcription companies and hence is not concerned particularly with the number of times the transcription is used by the lessee. It is this plan which the musicians union has adopted in connection with the television industry.

The second aspect of the problem is a major point of contention. Over the last decade there has been a gradual decline in the number of staff musicians employed by radio stations in the United States. To a larger extent, the independent stations have depended on records for the musical portion of their schedules and the affiliated stations have supplemented programs based on records with programs supplied by the network. It is likely that if this trend continues the union will give more attention to the matter. The union, however, has not been able to gain any control over the juke box operators.

Technological displacement problems seem to be less important to the musicians union today than at any time in the last 25 years. An adjustment has been made or a compromise has been reached along many fronts. Yet as the future is envisaged several potential strike questions loom forth. First, a few locals already have begun to exert pressure on the networks to reduce the amount of time allotted to records and transcriptions. The radio stations have resisted this demand forcefully. The industry thus far has been free from any limitation on the use of records and seems ready to take a strike rather than give way on this issue.

Secondly, the growing use of the kinescope may raise a serious issue. The kinescope, which for television corresponds to the record in the radio industry, is a motion picture of a television program. By building up a library of kinescopes it would be possible for a TV station to operate a balanced schedule of programs without employing musicians. The AFM has been able to negotiate agreements with the TV networks that when kinescopes are used the networks will allocate five per cent of the income derived to a fund established for the benefit of musicians. If the networks should decide not to renew such contract provisions in the future it seems that a strike against them is inevitable.

Thirdly, the union has begun to negotiate agreements along similar lines for the use of regular motion pictures over television. The union will try to prevent the motion picture film industry or the television stations from presenting over video the music of any film unless a payment is made to the music performance trust fund. The AFM also must continue to oppose the reuse of motion picture sound tracks in new pictures.

If the volume of unemployment among musicians becomes high, the American Federation of Musicians may be expected to take a stronger stand on some technological issues. Yet the union must recognize that as long as it generally admits to membership any person who claims to be a musician, the problem of unemployment may never be solved. Individuals are inclined to join the union when they know that the union provides for its unemployed. Everybody who can play an instrument should not be classified as a professional musician. Persistently high unemployment among musicians suggests that there are too many of them and that some persons who consider themselves to be professional musicians should be retrained.

Some musical critics have supported the contention of the union that excessive use of mechanical devices to replace live musicians somehow must be blocked; otherwise a reduction in the quality of musical performance eventually would take place because persons would have less incentive to study music. The ultimate result of such a situation would be a blow to cultural progress. Although this argument has some merit, the economic system in the United States leaves such decisions in the hands of the public. The people must choose, through their monetary outlays, the form of music they wish to hear.

The musicians union has accepted the principle that in a democracy labor cannot permanently stifle technological progress. The decision by the union is wise. The public, however, must recognize that technological change must come about through a smooth adjustment without seriously disrupting the lives of many workers. Stuart Chase concluded a study of the problem of technology by saying: "The machine of itself brings certain dangers and certain benefits. To my mind the latter outweigh the former."[4] If machines are used with discretion they serve to contribute greatly to the welfare of mankind.

NOTES

CHAPTER I

1. Cecil Johns, "The Stony Road to Unionism," *International Musician*, July 1946, p. 17.
2. *International Musician*, April 1950, p. 30.
3. Oscar Ameringer, *If You Don't Weaken*, 1940, p. 49.
4. *International Musician*, May 1907, p. 1.
5. *Ibid.*, January 1946, pp. 1, 15.
6. *American Musician*, May 1, 1898, p. 3.
7. The biographical facts in Weber's life as detailed by the union on different occasions show marked variation. Even the year of his birth cannot be decisively established. See *International Musician*, July 1925, p. 2 and January 1951, p. 7.
8. *Ibid.*, July 1927, p. 3.
9. *New York Sun*, July 17, 1904, p. 7:3.
10. John R. Commons, "Types of American Labor Unions—The Musicians of St. Louis and New York," *Quarterly Journal of Economics*, May 1906, p. 419.

CHAPTER II

1. *Christian Science Monitor*, March 18, 1922, p. 14:1 and *New York Times*, April 21, 1918, p. 8:3.
2. *Kunze* v. *Weber*, 197 App. Div. 319, 323, May 27, 1921 (Appellate Division, New York Supreme Court).
3. *Musical Mutual Protective Union* v. *Weber* (New York Supreme Court), *New York Law Journal*, October 4, 1922, p. 41:3.
4. *New York Tribune*, December 20, 1893, p. 7:1 and December 23, 1893, p. 9:1.
5. Walter Damrosch, *My Musical Life*, 1923, pp. 212-14.
6. *Philadelphia Public Ledger*, December 14, 1908.
7. *International Musician*, July 1927, p. 1.
8. 47 Stat. 67, March 17, 1932.
9. The ban on contract labor was ordered on August 7, 1929 in P. C. 1413 and its suspension came on April 11, 1947 in P. C. 1329. See *Statutory Orders and Regulations of Canada, Consolidation*, 1949, Volume II, pp. 2183-84.

10. *Official Opinions of the Attorneys-General of the United States,* Volume 27, pp. 90-95.
11. 39 Stat. 166, 188-89, June 3, 1916.
12. *Official Proceedings of the Annual Convention of the American Federation of Musicians,* 1904, p. 76.

CHAPTER III

1. Westbrook Pegler, "Thieves with Union Cards," *Collier's,* January 9, 1943, p. 30.
2. Bruce Dennis, "He Was Always Good at Arithmetic," *The Saturday Evening Post,* October 12, 1940, p. 13.
3. *International Musician,* April 1922, p. 3.
4. Bruce Dennis, *op. cit.,* p. 49.
5. *Ibid.*
6. *Rizzo, Belcaster* v. *Petrillo,* Records of Clerk, Circuit Court of Cook County, Case B 281, 594, December 19, 1933; cited in Twentieth Century Fund, *How Collective Bargaining Works,* 1942, p. 850.
7. Robert Coughlan, "Petrillo," *Life,* August 3, 1942, p. 74.
8. Geoffrey Parsons, Jr. and Robert M. Yoder, "Petrillo: Mussolini of Music," *The American Mercury,* November 1940, p. 285.
9. *International Musician,* July 1949, p. 10.
10. *Official Proceedings of the Annual Convention of the American Federation of Musicians,* 1950, pp. 95-99.
11. A description of the Chicago local may be found in Twentieth Century Fund, *How Collective Bargaining Works* 1942, pp. 848-66, 868. This is a section in the chapter on Chicago Service Trades, written by C. Lawrence Christenson.
12. Robert Coughlan, *op. cit.,* p. 70.
13. *New York Times,* January 14, 1943, p. 9:5, 6.
14. A good description of Petrillo by an artist who painted his portrait may be found in *International Musician,* December 1949, p. 27.
15. *Restrictive Union Practices of the American Federation of Musicians,* Hearings before the Committee on Education and Labor, House of Representatives, 1948 (80th Congress, 2nd Session), p. 308.

CHAPTER IV

1. *International Musician,* July 1929, p. 1.
2. See *ibid.,* June 1930, p. 17.

3. *Ibid.,* May 1928, p. 21.
4. *Ibid.,* November 1929, pp. 9-10.
5. *New York Daily News,* December 7, 1931, p. 22:3.
6. *Official Proceedings of the Annual Convention of the American Federation of Musicians,* 1932, p. 188.
7. *New York Times,* June 13, 1937, p. 1:4.
8. *Official Proceedings of the Annual Convention of the American Federation of Musicians,* 1951, p. 131.
9. *Waring* v. *WDAS Broadcasting Station, Inc.,* 194 Atl. 631, October 8, 1937.
10. *RCA Mfg. Co., Inc.* v. *Whiteman,* 114 F. 2d 86, CCA 2, July 25, 1940; affirmed by the U. S. Supreme Court, 311 U.S. 712, December 16, 1940.
11. *International Musician,* October 1927, p. 22.
12. Quoted from the *Chicago Tribune* in the *International Musician,* January 1937, p. 13.
13. *International Musician,* September 1916, p. 9; see also *ibid.,* October 1914, p. 8.
14. *Ibid.,* May 1938, p. 1.

CHAPTER V

1. *Use of Mechanical Reproduction of Music,* Hearings before a Subcommittee of the Committee on Interstate Commerce, United States Senate, 1942 (77th Congress, 2nd Session), p. 110.
2. *Restrictive Union Practices of the American Federation of Musicians,* Hearings before the Committee on Education and Labor, House of Representatives, 1948 (80th Congress, 2nd Session), p. 371.
3. *Official Journal,* Local 802, Associated Musicians of Greater New York, American Federation of Musicians, July 1940, p. 9.
4. American Federation of Musicians, *Constitution, By-Laws, and Standing Resolutions,* 1947, p. 20.
5. *Ibid.,* p. 8.
6. Figures have been obtained from various union sources. For some of the earlier years, conflicting figures may be found.
7. Figures on employment and earnings of musicians engaged in the motion picture industry are reported by the union. See *Official Proceedings of the Annual Convention of the American Federation of Musicians,* 1951, pp. 132-33, for the statistics for 1949.
8. *International Musician,* June 1927, p. 1.

9. *National Broadcasting Company, Inc.*, 59 NLRB 478, November 24, 1944 (certification), and 61 NLRB 161, March 31, 1945 (order to bargain).
10. *National Labor Relations Board* v. *National Broadcasting Co., Inc.*, 150 F.2d 895, 900, CCA 2, July 27, 1945.
11. *International Musician*, August 1948, p. 4.
12. *Ibid.*, October 1949, p. 7.
13. *New York Times*, October 1, 1949, p. 2:3. See also *Time*, October 10, 1949, p. 92.
14. *New York Times*, October 5, 1949, p. 24:1.
15. *International Musician*, September 1950, p. 11.
16. *Opera on Tour, Inc.* v. *Joseph N. Weber*, 285 N. Y. 348, 357, April 24, 1941. This decision overruled the Appellate Division of the Supreme Court, 17 N.Y.S.2d 144, January 26, 1940, which in turn had overruled the decision of the Supreme Court, 170 Misc. 272, January 24, 1939.
17. *Bartels* v. *Birmingham*, 332 U.S. 126, June 23, 1947.
18. *Official Journal, Allegro*, Local 802, Associated Musicians of Greater New York, May 1948, p. 6. But see *ibid.*, March 1952, p. 13, regarding responsibility for unemployment compensation taxes.
19. *International Musician*, May 1949, p. 8.
20. *Ibid.*, March 1935, p. 8.
21. *New York Times*, January 18, 1949, p. 17:5.
22. *International Musician*, November 1947, p. 16.

CHAPTER VI

1. *Official Proceedings of the Annual Convention of the American Federation of Musicians*, 1951, pp. 7-34.
2. *Investigation of So-Called "Rackets,"* Hearings before a Subcommittee of the Committee on Commerce, United States Senate, Volume II, Part 1, 1934 (73rd Congress, 2nd Session).
3. *Official Journal*, Local 802, Associated Musicians of Greater New York, American Federation of Musicians, February 1945, p. 13.
4. See *New York Times*, June 28, 1948, p. 15:1 and March 18, 1949, p. 33:1.
5. *Gamble Enterprises, Inc.*, 92 NLRB 1528, January 24, 1951; reversed by *Gamble Enterprises, Inc.* v. *National Labor Relations Board*, 196 F. 2d 61, CCA 6, May 9, 1952.
6. *New York World-Telegram*, January 8, 1942, p. 17:1.
7. 1939 Laws of New York 2151, June 13, 1939.
8. *International Musician*, January 1950, p. 35.

9. *New York Times,* September 12, 1946, p. 9:5.
10. *Hotel Association of St. Louis,* 92 NLRB 1388, January 17, 1951.
11. The text of the decision is printed in *Official Journal, Allegro,* Local 802, Associated Musicians of Greater New York, October 1950, p. 5.
12. *Ibid.,* May 1951, p. 28.
13. The membership figures have been taken from the records of the international union or of the local union.
14. *New York Times,* December 7, 1949, p. 1:6.
15. Robert Coughlan, "Petrillo," *Life,* August 3, 1942, p. 76.

CHAPTER VII

1. *New York Times,* August 14, 1940, p. 21:8.
2. See *AGMA, Official Organ of the American Guild of Musical Artists, Inc.,* July-August 1937, p. 4 and September-October 1937, p. 4. The union involved was the Grand Opera Artists Association of America.
3. *New York Times,* August 30, 1940, p. 21:8.
4. *Time,* September 2, 1940, p. 45.
5. *AGMA* v. *AFM,* 23 N.Y.S.2d 947, November 19, 1940.
6. *AGMA* v. *Petrillo,* 24 N.Y.S.2d 854, January 24, 1941.
7. *AGMA* v. *Petrillo,* 286 N.Y. 226, July 29, 1941.
8. *International Musician,* June 1942, p. 25.
9. *Ibid.,* June 1906, p. 8.
10. *New York Telegraph,* April 18, 1919; see Moses Smith, *Koussevitzky,* 1947, p. 141.
11. John T. Morse, Jr., "Henry Lee Higginson," *Harvard Graduates' Magazine,* March 1920, p. 391.
12. *New York Times,* August 14, 1940, p. 21:8.
13. *Boston Globe,* September 23, 1941; see Moses Smith, *op. cit.,* p. 318.
14. *New York Times,* December 15, 1942, p. 24:7.

CHAPTER VIII

1. *Use of Mechanical Reproduction of Music,* Hearings before a Subcommittee of the Committee on Interstate Commerce, United States Senate, 1942 (77th Congress, 2nd Session), p. 3.
2. *United States* v. *American Federation of Musicians,* 318 U.S. 741, February 15, 1943, affirming 47 F. Supp. 304, October 14, 1942.

3. *International Musician*, July 1908, p. 8.
4. *RCA Mfg. Co. Inc.* v. *Whiteman*, 114 F.2d 86, CCA 2, July 25, 1940; affirmed 311 U.S. 712, December 16, 1940.
5. These hearings were held on January 12, 13, and 14, 1943. The record was never published.
6. *New York Herald Tribune*, January 14, 1943, p. 14:2.
7. *Electrical Transcription Mfrs.*, 16 War Lab. Rep. 369, June 15, 1944; the decision of the NWLB to take jurisdiction was made on July 20, 1943, 10 War Lab. Rep. 157.
8. *Interference with Broadcasting of Noncommercial Educational Programs*, Hearings before the Committee on Interstate and Foreign Commerce, House of Representatives, 1945 (79th Congress, 1st Session), p. 16.
9. *Time*, November 20, 1944, p. 21.
10. *Official Proceedings of the Annual Convention of the American Federation of Musicians*, 1951, pp. 128-29.
11. *Ibid.*, 1949, p. 145.

CHAPTER IX

1. *New York Times*, July 21, 1942, p. 15:2.
2. *International Musician*, January 1944, p. 10.
3. *New York Times*, February 9, 1945, p. 17:6.
4. *Ibid.*, February 24, 1945, p. 13:3.
5. *Interference with Broadcasting of Noncommercial Educational Programs*, Hearings before the Committee on Interstate and Foreign Commerce, House of Representatives, 1945 (79th Congress, 1st Session).
6. *New York Times*, December 15, 1940, p. 1:2.
7. *Ibid.*, April 21, 1944, p. 1:2.
8. *Congressional Record*, 79th Congress, 2nd Session, Volume 92, p. 1553.
9. 60 Stat. 89, April 16, 1946.
10. *New York Times*, May 29, 1946, p. 4:4.
11. *Ibid.*, June 5, 1946, p. 14:1.
12. *Ibid.*, December 3, 1946, p. 34:2.
13. *Ibid.*, June 24, 1947, p. 5:6, 7.
14. The District Court handed down its decision on December 2, 1946 in *United States* v. *Petrillo*, 68 F. Supp. 845; the Supreme Court ruled on June 23, 1947 in *United States* v. *Petrillo*, 332 U.S. 1.
15. *United States* v. *Petrillo*, 75 F. Supp. 176, January 14, 1948.
16. *New York Times*, June 10, 1947, p. 1:6. Another version

of the threat, less favorable to Petrillo, is given by Wellington Roe. See *Juggernaut,* p. 212.
17. The code is reproduced in a Congressional document. See *Restrictive Union Practices of the American Federation of Musicians,* Hearings before the Committee on Education and Labor, House of Representatives, 1948 (80th Congress, 2nd Session), pp. 363-65.

Chapter X

1. 61 Stat. 136, 157-58, section 302 (c) (5), June 23, 1947.
2. *National Labor Relations Board* v. *E. C. Atkins & Co.,* 331 U.S. 398, 403, May 19, 1947.
3. *New York Times,* June 4, 1946, p. 18:3.
4. *Ibid.,* July 25, 1948, II, 5:1.
5. *Official Proceedings of the Annual Convention of the American Federation of Musicians,* 1949, pp. 103-4.
6. The various contracts with the recording and transcription companies and the legal opinions of the government officials are included *ibid.,* pp. 152-86.
7. *International Musician,* July 1949, pp. 11-12.
8. *New York Times,* October 25, 1945, p. 23:4.
9. *International Musician,* April 1951, pp. 16, 33.
10. The various contracts may be found in *Official Proceedings of the Annual Convention of the American Federation of Musicians,* 1951, pp. 94-123. See also *International Musician,* July 1950, p. 7 and *New York Times,* June 10, 1951, II, 3:1 and June 18, 1950, II, 13:6.
11. *Investigation of James C. Petrillo and the American Federation of Musicians,* House of Representatives, Report No. 1162, December 15, 1947 (80th Congress, 1st Session), p. 6.
12. *Investigation of James C. Petrillo, the American Federation of Musicians, et al.,* Hearings before the Special Subcommittee of the Committee on Education and Labor, House of Representatives, 1947 (80th Congress, 1st Session), p. 185.
13. *Ibid.,* p. 260.
14. *Investigation of James C. Petrillo and the American Federation of Musicians,* op. cit., p. 12.
15. *Restrictive Union Practices of the American Federation of Musicians,* Hearings before the Committee on Education and Labor, House of Representatives, 1948 (80th Congress, 2nd Session), p. 114.

16. *Ibid.*, p. 361.
17. *Ibid.*, p. 216.
18. *Ibid.*, p. 101.
19. *New York Times,* January 10, 1950, p. 1:6 and January 11, 1950, p. 11:1.

CHAPTER XI

1. *Official Proceedings of the Annual Convention of the American Federation of Musicians,* 1950, p. 92.
2. *International Musician,* August 1950, pp. 7, 34.
3. 35 Stat. 1075-76, March 4, 1909.
4. Stuart Chase, *Men and Machines,* 1929, p. 335.

BIBLIOGRAPHY

GENERAL SOURCES

Business Week
International Musician
Local 802, Associated Musicians of Greater New York, American Federation of Musicians, *Official Journal, Allegro*
New York Times
New York Times Index
Newsweek
Official Proceedings of the Annual Convention of the American Federation of Musicians
Time

BOOKS

Carpenter, Paul S., *Music, an Art and a Business,* 1950 (Chapter 7—In Union There Is Petrillo, pp. 137-49)
Roe, Wellington, *Juggernaut,* 1948 (Chapter 16—G-Clef Caesar, pp. 205-19)
Twentieth Century Fund, *How Collective Bargaining Works,* 1942 (Chapter 15—Chicago Service Trades by C. Lawrence Christenson: section 4, The Musicians of Chicago, pp. 848-66, 868)

GOVERNMENT DOCUMENTS

Electrical Transcription Mfrs., June 15, 1944, 16 War Lab. Rep. 369-99
Interference with Broadcasting of Noncommercial Educational Programs, Hearings before the Committee on Interstate and Foreign Commerce, House of Representatives, 79 Congress, 1 Session, February 22, 23, May 8, 10, 1945
Investigation of James C. Petrillo and the American Federation of Musicians, House of Representatives, Report No. 1162, 80 Congress, 1 Session, December 15, 1947
Investigation of James C. Petrillo, the American Federation of Musicians, et al., Hearings before the Special Subcommittee of the Committee on Education and Labor, House of Repre-

sentatives, 80 Congress, 1 Session, June 17, 18, 19, July 7, 8, August 4, 5, 6, 7, 1947

Investigation of So-Called "Rackets," Hearings before a Subcommittee of the Committee on Commerce, United States Senate, 73 Congress, 2 Session, Volume II, Part 1, January 31, 1934

Prohibiting Certain Coercive Practices Affecting Radio Broadcasting, House of Representatives, Report No. 1508, 79 Congress, 2 Session, January 29, 1946; Part 2 (minority views), February 8, 1946

Restrictive Union Practices of the American Federation of Musicians, Hearings before the Committee on Education and Labor, House of Representatives, 80 Congress, 2 Session, January 13, 14, 15, 16, 19, 21, 22, 1948

Use of Mechanical Reproduction of Music, Hearings before a Subcommittee of the Committee on Interstate Commerce, United States Senate, 77 Congress, 2 Session, September 17, 18, 21, 1942

MAGAZINE ARTICLES

Beatty, Jerome, "Hard-Boiled Maestro," *American Magazine,* October 1940, pp. 30-31, 130-31

Commons, John R., "Types of American Labor Unions—The Musicians of St. Louis and New York," *Quarterly Journal of Economics,* May 1906, pp. 419-42

Coughlan, Robert, "Petrillo," *Life,* August 3, 1942, pp. 68-70, 72, 74, 76

Countryman, Vern, "The Organized Musicians," *University of Chicago Law Review,* Autumn 1948, pp. 56-85 and Winter 1949, pp. 239-297

Dennis, Bruce, "He Was Always Good at Arithmetic," *The Saturday Evening Post,* October 12, 1940, pp. 12-13, 49-50, 52, 57

Lunde, Anders S., "The American Federation of Musicians and the Recording Ban," *Public Opinion Quarterly,* Spring 1948, pp. 45-56

Markey, Morris, "What Petrillo's Victory Means to You," *Liberty,* May 19, 1945, pp. 24-25, 68-69

Parsons, Geoffrey, Jr. and Robert M. Yoder, "Petrillo: Mussolini of Music," *The American Mercury,* November 1940, pp. 281-87

Pegler, Westbrook, "Thieves with Union Cards," *Collier's,* January 9, 1943, pp. 21, 30

"Petrillo, James Caesar," *Current Biography,* 1940, pp. 650-52

INDEX